Cambridge Elements ≡

Elements in the Philosophy of Religion
edited by
Yujin Nagasawa
University of Birmingham

FEMINISM, RELIGION AND PRACTICAL REASON

Beverley Clack
Oxford Brookes University

CAMBRIDGE
UNIVERSITY PRESS

CAMBRIDGE
UNIVERSITY PRESS

University Printing House, Cambridge CB2 8BS, United Kingdom

One Liberty Plaza, 20th Floor, New York, NY 10006, USA

477 Williamstown Road, Port Melbourne, VIC 3207, Australia

314–321, 3rd Floor, Plot 3, Splendor Forum, Jasola District Centre,
New Delhi – 110025, India

103 Penang Road, #05–06/07, Visioncrest Commercial, Singapore 238467

Cambridge University Press is part of the University of Cambridge.

It furthers the University's mission by disseminating knowledge in the pursuit of
education, learning, and research at the highest international levels of excellence.

www.cambridge.org
Information on this title: www.cambridge.org/9781108796866
DOI: 10.1017/9781108859653

First published 2021

A catalogue record for this publication is available from the British Library.

ISBN 978-1-108-79686-6 Paperback
ISSN 2399-5165 (online)
ISSN 2515-9763 (print)

Feminism, Religion and Practical Reason

Elements in the Philosophy of Religion

DOI: 10.1017/9781108859653
First published online: November 2021

Beverley Clack
Oxford Brookes University

Author for correspondence: Beverley Clack, bclack@brookes.ac.uk

Abstract: Pamela Sue Anderson's *A Feminist Philosophy of Religion* (1998) and Grace Jantzen's *Becoming Divine: Towards a Feminist Philosophy of Religion* (1998) set the tone for subsequent feminist philosophies of religion. This Element builds upon the legacy of their investigations, revisiting and extending aspects of their work for a contemporary context struggling with the impact of 'post-truth' forms of politics. Reclaiming the power of collective action felt in religious community and the importance of the struggle for truth enables a changed perspective on the world, itself necessary to realise the feminist desire for more flourishing forms of life and relationships crucial to feminist philosophy of religion.

Keywords: feminism, truth, evil, religion, flourishing

ISBNs: 9781108796866 (PB), 9781108859653 (OC)
ISSNs: 2399-5165 (online), 2515-9763 (print)

Contents

Introduction

Some twenty years have passed since the publication of the first books dedicated explicitly to Feminist Philosophy of Religion. Published in 1998, Pamela Sue Anderson's *A Feminist Philosophy of Religion* and Grace Jantzen's *Becoming Divine: Towards a Feminist Philosophy of Religion* set the tone for subsequent feminist approaches to the field. This Element builds upon their legacy, developing and extending aspects of their work for a much-changed contemporary context.

That this task is necessary reflects the absence of these two philosophers, whose lives were cut short and whose investigations were, as a result, nowhere near complete. Philosophical investigations, by their very nature, are rarely finished, yet the sense of these women dying in the middle of conversations they had opened up is palpable. Jantzen died in 2006 at the age of fifty-seven, the first in a series of six books she intended to write on 'Death and the Displacement of Beauty' having been published in 2004. Jeremy Carrette's memorial article (2006) offers a tantalising flavour of where she might have gone in her thinking had she lived. Anderson died in 2017 at the age of sixty-one. A dominant theme in her work at the time was human vulnerability. A piece by her, read in absentia at the British Academy conference on 'Vulnerability and the Politics of Care' a month before she died, reflected the ruthlessly honest eye she was bringing to this theme.[1]

My enquiry is shaped by three aspects of their work.

The first is Anderson's unwillingness to throw over entirely the structures of philosophy of religion, which offers the possibility of an open feminist philosophy based upon a rich combination of sources. She conducts a philosophical conversation with a range of partners: some women, some men; some feminist, some not; some philosophical, some theological, some literary.

Expanding the range of conversation partners is reflected in the second aspect of her work that influences my approach. Anderson explores the ethical potential of philosophy of religion. Philosophy of religion is a form of critical practice concerned with the investigation of truth-claims. The established content of the subject clusters around arguments designed to establish (or reject) the reasonableness of belief in God; in its analytic form its account of religion is grounded in the investigation of theism and the attempt to establish (or to reject) the truth-claims attending to this concept. Anderson's feminist approach is significant as she takes this notion into the realm of practical living. Shaped by feminist concerns, philosophy of religion 'no longer focuses strictly on epistemological

---

[1] See 'Silencing and speaker vulnerability: undoing an oppressive form of (wilful) ignorance', in Pelagia Goulimari's collection (2021, 34–43) published in Anderson's memory.

questions to do with belief, knowledge, or the truth of a claim that "God exists", or that "we are free agents"' (Anderson 2009, 124). Rather, it is to be understood as a critical discipline that is also a practical endeavour. To adopt this approach is to expand the range of philosophers' reflections on God and agency by 'thinking freedom, acting virtuously and making reflective (aesthetic) judgements which would be creative spirituality' (2009, 125).

This suggests something of the distinctive feminist approach to philosophy of religion, and leads to the third theme drawn from the work of these two foremothers. Philosophy of religion is shaped by both women as a form of practice that enables the flourishing life. The question of what it is to flourish is central to Jantzen's approach. She argues that this involves attending to birth and natality (neglected as philosophical themes, she contends, because of their association 'only' with women). Taking seriously these features enables a different way of considering the focus and values of human life from one centred on death and mortality. Anderson, in similar vein, suggests that the aim of feminist philosophy of religion is to cultivate 'the love of life' (2009).

How to nurture the conditions for a flourishing life drives my enquiry. Rosemary Radford Ruether's pithy definition of feminism as the promotion of that which affirms 'the full humanity of women' (Ruether 1983) is central to my philosophy of religion. It explains the necessary starting point – namely, the identification of and resistance to the structures and attitudes that historically denied women's full humanity – and the development of a philosophy of religion that engages with themes beyond the specific discussion of sex and gender. If women *really are* 'full human beings', the reflections they develop should be capable of informing what it means to flourish, not just as a woman but also as a human being.

As I develop my feminist philosophy of religion, a number of problems must be addressed. A central contention of womanists and black feminists[2] is that 'white feminists', benefitting from the structures of western liberal societies, consistently ignore the power of collective action and thus the possibilities of religious community for shaping the lives and resistance of oppressed peoples. The concern of white feminists with personal autonomy does not allow space, it is claimed, for an understanding of religion as a collective endeavour shaping political action (Grant 1989; Armour 1999). Tina Beattie's (2004) critique of

---

[2] For discussion of 'womanist' and 'black feminist', see Patricia Hill Collins (1996). Collins cites Alice Walker's four features of womanism: i) a womanist is 'a black feminist or feminist of colour'; ii) womanism resists separatism and is committed to the survival and wholeness of men *and* women; iii) a womanist loves music, dance, struggle, spirit, food, her people, her self; and iv) the connection with feminism: 'womanist is to feminist as purple is to lavender'. 'On some basic level, Walker herself uses the two terms [womanist and black feminist] as being virtually interchangeable' (Collins 1996, 10).

feminist philosophy of religion likewise draws attention to the problems of individualistic feminisms, framed by an unacknowledged Protestantism concerned with establishing 'right belief'. Analysing the work of Jantzen and Anderson, Beattie identifies an implicit liberalism beneath their apparent differences. The emphasis on the critique of belief and the attention given to individual liberation limits, Beattie claims, the significance of the feminist approach for the philosophical investigation of religion. For Beattie, both Anderson and Jantzen fail to address the aesthetic and communal aspects of religion and its practice: a lacuna her Catholic approach attempts to fill.

In what follows, I build upon the foundation provided by Anderson and Jantzen, while taking seriously the force of these criticisms. My feminist philosophy of religion is defined thus:

Firstly, I understand feminism as a political and practical movement. It is a way of thinking and – crucially – acting, requiring liberating forms of praxis extending beyond the concerns of the self towards a collective response to (primarily but not only) sex-based forms of injustice.

Secondly, I offer a feminist philosophy *of religion* that recognises its relationship to feminist theology. The critique of religion influenced feminist theological enquiry from its earliest days (Stanton 1895; Daly 1986 [1973]). For feminist theologians like Daphne Hampson (1990; 1996; 2002), the critique of 'patriarchal' forms of religion reveals that, far from being an innocent phenomenon, religious systems of belief, and the institutions that support them, provide tools that, over the centuries, have been highly effective for the oppression of women. Not all agree with this analysis (Ruether 1983; 2012; Coakley 2002; Haynes 2014a), and I suggest something of the possibilities of religion for shaping liberating forms of life as we proceed. Recent work in the philosophy of religion suggests the need to reflect upon 'living religion' (Hewitt and Scrutton 2018), locating analysis of religion in the lived experience of religious communities (Burley 2020), rather than solely in assessment of accounts of God that can appear overly abstracted from the living out of a religious faith. The desire for more nuanced engagements with the phenomenon of religion is, similarly, reflected in what follows, and, here, the reflections of black feminist and women theologians are most helpful for the development of a feminist philosophy of religion.

Drawing upon both negative and positive strands in the feminist analysis of religion, I recognise the problems of patriarchal history for religious traditions, but also the possibilities of reclaiming the power of collective action felt in religious community. The account of 'the religious' that I pursue enables the kind of diversity and pluralism that political theorists like Hannah Arendt (1998 [1958]) deemed necessary for human flourishing, and that has possibilities for shaping a more just world. Religious practice allows for the development of a changed perspective on the world and the place of human beings within it. Here is the possibility of renewed connection with others and the world that makes possible richer forms of living: an aim that connects liberating forms of religious practice with the preoccupations of feminists.

1 Rethinking Feminism

1.1 The Disappearance (and Re-emergence?) of Feminist Philosophy of Religion

Writing a feminist philosophy of religion in 2021 requires some explanation: not least because an impartial observer might note the lack of titles announcing themselves in this way, concluding that this ideological starting point is no longer relevant in the Brave New World of (fluid) gender identities that proliferates in the intellectual scene of the second decade of the twenty-first century.

An historical overview proves illuminating. The appearance of Anderson's and Jantzen's monographs in feminist philosophy of religion at the end of the 1990s set in train a series of exciting developments. New collections were published (Anderson and Clack 2004); designated panels were convened at prestigious international conferences;[3] textbooks and guides to the subject routinely included reflection on feminist approaches (Taliaferro and Griffiths 2003). It was impossible not to conclude that addressing the role of women in the sphere of religion, and the significance of gender for framing philosophical accounts of religion, was opening up new vistas for philosophy of religion.

The breadth of the approaches offered by Anderson and Jantzen suggests something of the richness of the field as it developed during these years. Anderson's book supplemented traditional methods of analytic philosophy of religion with sources drawn from the 'Continental' intellectual tradition. Kant, and Anderson's extensive knowledge of his ethics (Anderson 1993), sat alongside the theories of Luce Irigaray, Julia Kristeva and Michèle Le Doeuff. Anderson's method of expansion created a place for desire and the emotions in the philosophical discussion of religion (Anderson 1998, 171–6). She pointed out how the habitual connection between women and desire led to a model of religion where the emotions were routinely excluded. Bringing together reason and emotion, philosophy and yearning, suggested a different way of shaping the conversations philosophers could have about religious beliefs and practices (1998, 165–206). Acknowledging the place of emotions in religious sensibility was as important as subjecting beliefs to rational analysis.

---

[3] The American Academy of Religion Conference at Philadelphia (19–22 November 2005) included the first panel dedicated to Feminist Philosophy of Religion.

Jantzen's approach appears more radical, not least because she rejects 'mainstream' philosophy of religion. She describes a discipline shaped by values identified historically with the male and masculinity. 'Necrophilia' (1998, 8) is at the heart of analytic philosophy of religion: death as the destroyer of human agency may be feared, but it is also desired. Faced with a philosophical practice that is life-denying, and that excludes those aspects of life identified with the female, only a radically new philosophising will do. Jantzen turns to Continental philosophies to develop her approach. The weight they are made to carry is significantly more than is the case in Anderson's work. Anderson remains a Kantian when it comes to her ethics; Jantzen's chief conversation partner is Luce Irigaray. Employing psychoanalytic categories derived from Irigaray's work enables a feminist philosophy of religion that seeks to transform not just the discipline, but the practitioner, and, moreover, the world itself. The questions shaping Jantzen's enquiry shape philosophy as a transformational practice: What does it mean to flourish as a human being (Jantzen 1998, 156–70)? What do we need to establish trustworthy community (1998, 227–53)? What role should birth play in philosophy (1998, 144–54)? Whose problem is the 'problem of evil' (1998, 259–66)? The answers she proffers suggest as much the need for practical engagement with the struggles of human life as new theoretical frameworks. This aspect of her analysis more than almost anything else shapes my concern with developing a practical feminist philosophy of religion: ideas shape how we live.

This brief outline of Anderson and Jantzen's respective projects suggests something of the energy accompanying the early years of feminist philosophy of religion. It *felt* as if there was a fertile future for the feminist philosophical investigation of religion. So why the absence in 2021 of works in 'feminist philosophy of religion'? What went wrong? Alternatively, what went *right*? The use of feminist themes in philosophy of religion not declared as explicitly feminist suggests an implicit acceptance of many ideas driving the Analyses of Anderson and Jantzen during this creative period of philosophical exploration.

An article by Michelle Panchuk suggests this might be the case. In a collection that considers 'the lost sheep' of philosophy of religion – disability, gender, race and animals – Panchuk addresses the question of wholeness in tones that echo Anderson's love of life and Jantzen's flourishing. Panchuk's piece is not explicitly feminist, although she draws upon aspects of feminist work (not, though, the work of either Anderson or Jantzen). Panchuk envisages the body as the site of lived experience: a term peppering Anderson's text (1998, 99–100; 115; 179–80). Panchuk questions the supposed 'gender-neutrality' of analytic philosophy of religion, a crucial aspect of Anderson and Jantzen's critique (Anderson 1998, 16; Jantzen 1998, 28–32). Moreover, Panchuk develops a powerful argument for a philosophy of religion that engages with 'wholeness', a word resonating with Anderson's and Jantzen's projects for the cultivation of human flourishing. Panchuk's challenge, like theirs, is directed at the failure of analytic philosophers to engage with lived experience. Her article opens with her experience of presenting work on trauma to a conference of philosophers of religion:

> The prospect of discussing the sadistic abuse of a friend as if it had been inflicted on the abstract entities that populate philosophical thought experiments, rather than a flesh-and-blood child, made me feel sick – even morally suspect. I had exposed the wounds and souls of my friends and myself to being poked by those for whom analysis was merely an academic exercise, for whom nothing of import hung on the conclusion of the argument. These weren't bad people. They weren't even the source of my trepidation per se – disciplinary norms were. My project was philosophical. As such there was a tacit expectation that we would treat it as if it were neither personal nor political. (2019, 55)

The sense that there is something fundamentally wrong with the model of the human subject habitually used in philosophy of religion is apparent in Panchuk's painful words. The presence of challenging works like hers suggests it is no longer necessary to *foreground* feminist claims: these are taken as read. Anderson and Jantzen thus achieved their goal of creating a context for new and creative forms of philosophising.

Much can be said for this conclusion. 'Mainstreaming' feminism suggests that what matters is furthering the feminist commitment to justice in philosophy and philosophising. I have much sympathy with this claim, not least because it informs aspects of my approach. As noted in the introduction, feminism is that which promotes 'the full humanity of women', and as Pearl Cleage notes, women are thus 'capable of participation and leadership *in the full range of human activities* – intellectual, political, social, sexual, spiritual and economic' (in Collins 1996, 12; my emphasis).

Yet the dangers of ignoring sex- and gender-based discrimination are starkly illustrated in the experience of feminist activism. The suggestion that feminism had achieved its ends was embraced in the 'post-feminist' discourses of the 1990s (Haraway 1991; Gamble 1998). Old group identities and 'Grand Narratives' that previously shaped understandings of human life and experience no longer enabled liberation. The focus shifted from addressing the collective oppression of women to understanding liberation as required by *all* people in order for individual desires and hopes to be freed up (Hekman 2014, 113–46). Viewed from 2021, the shelving of an explicit feminism seems somewhat premature. The rise of populist politics worldwide, accompanied by conservative social agendas, has returned the question of women's liberation to the table.

In Poland, access to abortion was effectively banned by a ruling in October 2020 that terminations on the basis of foetal defects were 'unconstitutional'. In the USA, the election of Donald Trump as President in 2016 shocked many, not least because this occurred despite the production of a tape during the campaign of Trump boasting of his methods as a sexual predator. In the wake of this political earthquake, feminist activism saw something of a revival, the 'Me Too' movement exposing women's common experience of sexual harassment and violence in ways not so clearly articulated since the heady days of the 1970s and 1980s Women's Movement.[4]

If the shoots of a new feminist politics are emerging out of this febrile political scene, might there be a future for a feminist *philosophy of religion*? Can feminist philosophy of religion be reimagined through a connection to the everyday, encompassing modes of philosophising that have as their goal political and social transformation? To make such a move requires further investigation of feminist philosophy of religion's past. Excavating this past suggests something of what went wrong, while holding out the possibility of a renewed vision for a contemporary feminist philosophy of religion.

1.2 The Perennial Problem of Feminist Philosophy (of Religion)

My concern is to develop a *practical* feminist philosophy of religion. Immediately this raises questions of what it means to practise philosophy and, moreover, to engage as a philosopher with matters of religion.

A criticism long-levelled at feminist philosophy is that it is not 'real' philosophy. Feminists, it is claimed, are insufficiently objective when they engage in the work of critical analysis. To start from a feminist perspective is to locate one's philosophical investigations within a particular, politically determined space. One's philosophy is shaped by explicit identification of historic and continuing injustice against women; one's practice as a feminist philosopher aims at challenging this.

The history of feminist philosophical investigation reveals this political framing. Feminist philosophers consistently challenge the notion that there could be a way of philosophising that eschews one's ideological commitments and/or one's lived experience. A key feature of the so-called 'second wave' of feminist theorising was to draw attention to the 'masculinising' of reason.[5] A central text for this critical history is Genevieve Lloyd's *The Man of Reason* (1984), where 'Woman' emerges as a key category for western philosophising,

---

[4] See key texts from this period: Brownmiller 1975; Dworkin 1981; Cameron and Frazer 1987.

[5] The depiction of 'waves' of feminist enquiry is somewhat misleading. The past does not 'disappear', and we do well to remember this when considering the diversity of feminist approaches populating the contemporary scene (Browne 2014, 19; Nicholson 2010).

acting as a cipher for that which (masculine) Reason rejects. Language borrowed from ecofeminist theorising captures the resulting gendered binary perfectly: 'Woman' is to Nature as 'Man' is to Reason (Ortner 1972; Plumwood 1993). 'Woman' is connected with the body and the processes of reproduction, with feeling and emotion: features that exclude 'Her' from the attributes of rationality and dispassionate reflection routinely associated with 'Man'.

This construction continues to be felt in claims that feminist philosophy is 'too partial'. Dismissals of this kind implicitly accept the attributes of reason and detachment as central to the practice of philosophy without understanding the gendered history that shapes them. 'These' modes of reflecting are, apparently, general and impartial, while feminist philosophy is 'merely' partial and subjective. Explicit misogyny might be hard to find in contemporary philosophical publications, but Jennifer Saul's (2013) work on unconscious gender bias suggests how this dichotomy continues to operate in the construction of philosophical argument and the structures of the discipline itself. Men look and act like philosophers; women, it seems, don't.

This observation goes some way to explaining the dearth of women in the history of philosophy and its contemporary practice. Defined as that which is opposed to rational reflection – or, at the very least, as less capable of such reflection than the male – women have been excluded by their very ontology from the practices shaping the intellectual history of humanity. For feminist philosophers, it is not possible to engage with philosophical work without paying attention to the history of misogyny underpinning claims for apparently neutral philosophical positions.[6]

At the same time, feminist philosophy emerged from the historical struggles for women's rights and equality with men. Important thinkers in that history such as Gabrielle Suchon (1632–1703), Mary Wollstonecraft (1759–97) and Simone de Beauvoir (1908–86) cannot be understood without an awareness of the political struggles for women's dignity and equality that helped form their ideas. This historically grounded reflection means the feminist cannot ignore the meshing together of ideas and practice. There is an *interdependence* between thought and action (Collins 1990, 29), and feminist theorising makes this explicit. Adopting a feminist viewpoint requires more than taking on an ideological perspective: it shapes and informs the whole of one's life.

As a result, feminist philosophies are intimately connected to practical questions about how best to live in the world. This raises questions about the relationship between feminist enquiry and truth-claims. Can a feminist

---

[6] For examples of misogyny in the history of western philosophy, see Clack's 1999 anthology.

philosophy ignore questions of truth or objectivity? What happens if feminist ideas fail to cohere with matters of fact? Is there a way of framing the commitment to the liberation of all women – central to its historical formulation – that does not misrepresent the variety of perspectives possible for women, and the diverse ways in which the flourishing of different individual women and groups of women might be attained? Questions like these necessarily thread their way through the themes we will encounter.

At this point, the second theme of this Element comes into view. This is not simply about feminism, though that story and its possible futures are a necessary part of it. It is, rather, a feminist engagement with *religion*. If analytic philosophy of religion concerns itself with possible justifications for religious belief, the feminist approach to philosophy of religion directs attention to the constraints patriarchal religion places on women's lives. Like philosophy, the discussion of religion cannot proceed without understanding the way it has developed out of a history that enshrined male power through institutions and ideas, and where women's opportunities to shape political and intellectual life were as a result severely curtailed.

Feminist theology and philosophy of religion share deep roots: many of the ideas framing feminist philosophy of religion are drawn from earlier analyses by feminist theologians. The ideas of Mary Daly, a feminist theologian trained in philosophy, helped shape the first feminist philosophies of religion. Daly describes at length the uses of religion for constraining women's lives (Daly 1986 [1973]; 1978). Religious doctrines offer transcendent justifications for the exercise of earthly power: 'If God in "his" heaven is a father ruling "his" people, then it is in the nature of things and according to the divine plan and the order of the universe that society be male-dominated' (Daly 1986 [1973], 13). Deconstructing the all-too-human qualities of religion and its role in maintaining patriarchal society opens up a different set of questions for feminist philosophers of religion to those shaping the investigations of their colleagues. One of the most important concerns the extent to which being a feminist is – or is not – compatible with practising one of the religious traditions developing out of the patriarchal history Daly is at pains to expose.

While this suggests something of the distinctive path feminists take in their investigations of religion, there is common ground between feminist philosophers of religion and their apparently more neutral counterparts. With the analytic philosopher of religion, the feminist philosopher of religion engages in the analysis of religious beliefs, though with an emphasis on the way belief shapes action. In itself, this is not peculiar to feminism: RB Braithwaite (1971 [1955]) makes a similar connection in an intervention that remains influential (Hick 1989, 193–209). What makes the feminist perspective distinctive is the emphasis on gender: *masculine* theological language makes possible the maintenance of sexist perspectives.

This emphasis explains Hampson's (1990; 2002) rejection of religious traditions shaped by patriarchal history. Traditions formed in social contexts that enshrined sexual inequality perpetuate a sense of female inferiority: 'For a feminist to be a Christian is indeed for her to swallow a fishbone. It must stick in her throat' (Hampson 1996, 1). This trenchant claim has not gone unanswered, as Sarah Coakley, Julie Hopkins, Janet Martin Soskice, Jane Shaw and Nicola Slee make clear (Hampson 1996). For many women, the traditions Hampson wants them to reject provide liberating narratives for the framing of their lives.

The diversity of feminist religious perspectives highlights the malleable nature of religion. Religion is a multifaceted phenomenon. Rituals, rites and communal practices have just as significant roles to play as belief, a fact not lost on Amy Hollywood (2004), who, like Beattie, suggests the importance of attending to the practices of religion.

Here is a connection between feminism and religion not always identified by feminist critics of the latter, possibly because the secular framing of feminist politics does not make space for considering the ground shared with the religious. *Neither feminism nor religion can be reduced to ways of thinking, for both are grounded in and require specific forms of action.*

Explaining this oversight, Amy Newman suggests that feminist scholars have adopted an uncritical acceptance of the Marxist critique of religion. For Marx, religion acts as a justification of unjust power structures, providing a sop for human suffering, as well as pacifying feelings of outrage that might lead the oppressed to revolt against their masters. This rendition of the *effect* of holding to a set of religious beliefs informs feminist identifications of religious justifications for patriarchal social structures. Power and its exercise becomes a necessary part of the discussion of religion. If turning the gaze to the role of power is a helpful aspect of Marx's critique, Newman is not convinced by the adoption of his generalised account of what 'religion' is. Marx's definition of 'religion' is shaped by monolithic readings of Judaism and Christianity (Newman 1994, 20). Claims that there is only one way of reading Jewish or Christian texts or one form of religious practice in these traditions is far from the reality of religious diversity, and fails to engage with the lived experiences of those practising their faith. Newman hopes that feminists will challenge these inaccurate representations and 'turn from abstract and ideologically instigated constructions of "religion"', considering, instead, 'the actual self-understanding of particular persons or groups' (1994, 32).

Newman rightly draws attention to the problem of generalisation. Just as supposedly 'neutral' analytic philosophers of religion must avoid the tendency of engaging with 'religion' as if it were made manifest in only one way (thereby reducing 'religion' to belief in monotheism), feminists must be wary of suggesting only one model for feminist enquiry or action, thereby ignoring the multiplicity of ways in which women experience the world. The liberal tendency to universal claims and generalised constructions is a trap from which feminists do not always escape. A feminist philosophy of religion may well need to embrace the need for *philosophies* of *religions* in order to maintain a sense of complexity and nuance. It may not, however, be a case of *either* adopting general *or* particular forms of engagement with religion. There is value, I will suggest, in investigating 'religion' as a universal phenomenon, while maintaining the importance of engaging with specific faith practices. An understanding of religion as a form of human practice is helpful for seeking that which brings human beings together, and which connects them to their world. This possibility is returned to in Section 1.5.

1.3 False Generalisations and the Legacy of (Neo)Liberalism

So far, we have considered some pitfalls to avoid when setting out a revived feminist agenda for the philosophy of religion. The suggestion that philosophers of religion engage more explicitly with 'living religion' enables a more realistic engagement with the negative and positive dimensions that weave throughout the religious life and that are evident in the debates of feminist theology. Enabling a more complex reading of religion requires further investigation of some trenchant problems attending to feminist perspectives.

1.3.1 The Exclusions of Generalisation

The very notion of a 'feminist' approach to anything is not unproblematic. To speak of 'feminism' suggests a concern with the lived experiences of *all* women. Yet the history of the Women's Movement reveals the negative consequences of an account of 'women's experience' drawn only from the lives of white, middle class and affluent women.

Feminism's painful past is described in disturbing detail by black feminists. bell hooks' classic text on this theme, *Ain't I a Woman* (1982), exposes the failure of white women to support their black sisters during the struggles for emancipation and civil rights in the United States. Racism has rarely been addressed by feminists with the same intensity as sexism. The notion of a 'universal sisterhood' connecting all women seems flimsy at best when considered alongside the failure of white feminists to challenge the exclusions based upon the beliefs and practices of societies that accept – implicitly or explicitly – claims for white supremacy.

The title of hooks' book – 'Ain't I a Woman?' – comes from the refrain of freed slave Sojourner Truth in her speech to the Second Annual Convention of the Women's Rights Movement in Akron, Ohio, in 1851. White women in the crowd – women committed to advocating 'the rights of women' – thought it 'unseemly' that a black woman should address them. Truth's attempt to speak elicited cries of 'Don't let her speak! Don't let her speak!' (hooks 1982, 159). The desire for respectability, the hope of getting white men to support their cause, demanded – these white women believed – the silencing of black women. Truth did speak, and her words provided a powerful rebuttal to attempts at silencing her, and also to claims that women could not participate in public life because of their inherent weakness. Truth drew attention to her life as a slave: 'I have plowed, and planted, and gathered into barns, and no man could head me' (hooks 1982, 159). So much for the myth of the 'Angel in House': the delicate flower in need of male protection did not inform the treatment of black women, who were expected to do the hard physical labour on which white privilege depended. (Nor, we might add, did that image speak much to the experience of her white working class counterparts.) A broader understanding of what constitutes 'the lives of women' is required. 'Ain't I a woman?' Truth asks, in words that confront the feminist movement as much as they do the structures of male-dominated societies.

Truth's words show the power of women giving voice to the nature of their oppression and the desire for liberation, just as her words alert us to the problems of assuming there is one experience all women share. Race and class are as significant for shaping one's experience of the world as sex or gender identity, and as a result must be taken just as seriously. As hooks' analysis shows, to do this, the multilayered nature of oppression must be addressed. An uncomfortable truth is that white women may have more in common with – and be more invested in – the doctrines of white supremacy underpinning patriarchy than they do with those seeking to challenge it. For feminist activism to be powerful and broad-based, the intersections of race, class and sex in constructing oppression and the web of identity must be acknowledged (Crenshaw 2017; Collins and Bilge 2020). A feminism reflecting only the voices of those holding privileged places in society will not be good enough.

Ellen Armour's influential work (1999) on the race/gender divide highlights the problem of basing any feminist philosophy of religion on false generalisations of female identity. Armour exhorts white feminists to adopt more critical engagements with their own racial positioning. Race is not just an issue for black women. Blindness towards their own race and the privileges attending to white skin ensures that 'white feminism' passes off as a universal and all-encompassing feminist politics what is, in actuality, a partial feminism, based on the exclusion of black women.

Armour's analysis directs attention to the contested meaning of the word 'Woman'. Early feminist critiques of this construct exposed the gender stereo-typing lying beneath claims about the nature of 'Woman'. Armour goes further. Critiquing the stereotypes constructing 'Woman' has implications for a feminist politics. There is no one, unified form of female 'experience', just as there is no one, unified group of women. This means that any feminist politics must be far more complex than one based upon easy suggestions of what is required for 'women's' liberation. As a result, 'the task feminism faces involves recognising and negotiating the terms of the contest in ways that promote coalitions among those who would gather under its flag' (Armour 1999, 183). Falling back on false universals that ignore the diversity of women's experience must be avoided. Race – along with class and economic disadvantage – must be acknowledged *and embedded* in the actions of any movement aimed at women's flourishing.

The womanist critique of white feminism driving Armour's project does more than castigate white women for failing to engage with their unacknow-ledged privilege; it also opens up the question of how to engage with religion. If feminist approaches to religion are dominated by the necessity of critiquing the role it plays in maintaining oppressive structures – more than that, have seen it as a means of enshrining hierarchical distinction by employing notions of divine will – womanist theologians highlight the extent to which religious community provides vital support for those experiencing the oppressive structures of white supremacist society (Williams 1993). This suggests an alternative to the Marxist critique of religion. The power of collective action, the support of community, *is made possible* through the practices of religion.

Before pursuing this in more detail, it is worth bringing this claim into critical conversation with the dominant form individualism takes in contemporary western societies. The womanist critique of white feminism alerts us to uncrit-ical assumptions of group identities, yet it does more than this. Centring a feminist politics on claims for individual freedom is not necessarily the best way of framing human flourishing. The feminist philosophy of religion I advocate accepts the importance of community for framing life and experi-ence, while resisting attempts at romanticising the reality of community. Womanists and black feminists are clear-eyed about this complexity, as we shall see. Out of such readings, the possibilities (and challenges) of religious community become clear.

1.3.2 Liberalism and Individualism in Feminist Theorising

An important aspect of bell hooks' work highlights the erosion of class as a key category in the shaping of different forms of identity politics (hooks 2000). The championing of diversity in recent institutional and cultural initiatives largely focuses on issues arising from race, sex, gender and sexual orientation, rather than from economic inequalities enshrined through class hierarchies. The erosion of class requires discussion, for it suggests something of the power of liberal approaches to identity that are uncomfortable with accounts of political action based on collective identities.

An example from the history of the struggle for women's emancipation in the UK is helpful. The 1918 Representation of the People Act extended the franchise to women over thirty who were householders or the wives of householders, occupiers of property with an annual rent of £5, or who were university graduates. Middle class and propertied women were thus the beneficiaries of this extension of the franchise, at the expense of their less-well-off sisters (DiCenzo 2014). That this was the case highlights a tension between middle class and working class women in the movement for women's suffrage. According to RS Neale, the two senior Pankhursts – Emmeline and Christabel – were 'only interested in the class struggle for as long as it could assist them in the sex war for equality' (1967, 26). In support of this contention, Neale cites Sylvia Pankhurst's recollection of a conversation with her sister Christabel regarding Sylvia's East London Federation, a foundation committed to organising working women to achieve broad aims of sex and class liberation. Christabel saw a working women's movement as of no value in achieving the end of female emancipation: 'working women were the weakest portion of the sex ... "Surely it is a mistake to use the weakest for the struggle. We want picked women, the very strongest and most intelligent! You have your own ideas. We do not want that; we want our women to take their instructions and walk in step like an army"' (in Neale 1967, 26). Prejudices about the capabilities of working women imbue these words: the women's movement is to be directed by middle class women who 'know what they are doing'. The tensions between white and black women, revealed in the examples from American feminism, are mirrored in the class struggle. It is unwise to assume that feminist activism has been consistently shaped by the hopes of *all* women, even as it has militated for political change.

The erosion of difference and the prioritising of one vision of Woman can be located in the relationship between feminism and philosophical liberalism. The central liberal claim is that values can be identified that are applicable to all peoples, at all times, in all places. The well-lived life appears, as a result, to be universally applicable. Yet the vision of this life, invariably, reflects the experiences of the privileged white male. Seen against this backdrop, the aim of the feminist is equality with the male, rather than in challenging the ideals that shape male-dominated society and culture.

Emphasising intersectionality suggests one way out of this impasse: a nexus exists between race, sex, gender and class that forms identity. Oppression, read thus, cannot be reduced to one kind or condition, but reflects the realities of different contexts and experiences, and thus requires complex forms of feminism to achieve the work of liberation. For some, like Lois McNay (1992), the archaeological framework of Michel Foucault's ideas acts as a method for enabling this political aim. There is no one historical reality, as his exposure of diverse perspectives makes plain. Similarly, Judith Butler's ideas have been crucial for showing how attention to diverse forms of identity might shape feminist theorising.

There is, however, an aspect of the move to celebrate diversity that is not so helpful for the work of liberation required by women at the mercy of economic forces. Diversity can fragment into a disconnected individualism, and it is worth exploring the dominance of an economic model that has shaped the contemporary celebration of difference. Just as the intersectional approach gains traction, so *all* forms of identity are made subject to another universal principle. The Enlightenment image of human beings as rational agents is shaped by a new set of economic concerns, and a new kind of liberalism emerges: 'neoliberalism'.

Neoliberalism, the creed that has shaped the last forty or so years, emerges from the struggles of the 1970s. Faced with a number of political crises – industrial disputes and the OPEC oil crisis being foremost (Harvey 2005) – the old post-war consensus, framed by belief in an interventionist state, broke down. A new emphasis on market values emerged. Behind these economic policies, a new understanding of human identity was being forged. The individual was best understood as an economic unit; the old group identities of sex, race and class were rendered obsolete by the central task of self-definition in a marketplace. The individual was to be an 'entrepreneur of the self' (Lemke 2001, 199): free to be whosoever they wanted to be, free to 'create themselves'. Indeed, only those grasping the openness of these myriad opportunities would thrive in a world where to live well was associated with achieving economic success (Rose 1999).

The Global Financial Crisis of 2007/2008 and the Covid-19 Pandemic of 2020/2021 have challenged the usefulness of this model for economics and human relationships;[7] yet it is more difficult to dislodge the image of the

---

[7] See Peck 2010 and Mirowski 2014 for the effect of the former; Ellis *et al* 2020 for possible ramifications of the latter.

individual informing both. There is something attractive about modelling one-self as a lone subject, bravely attempting to 'stand out' from the world. This image suggests we are free to make of ourselves what we will. Group identities no longer anchor the political self: they can be overcome on the level playing field of 'opportunity' and 'the classless society'. Defining one's politics through experiences that attend to being *a woman* and that are shared with other women – making that identity fundamental to one's politics – looks quaint and old-fashioned when considered against this backdrop.

Feminism thus faces a pincer movement. On the one hand, it is accused of failing to engage adequately with the diversity of women's experience; on the other, in a world where the desires of the individual and the imperative of self-expression are central values, the very idea that there might be experiences that women share, simply by inhabiting societies historically created and maintained by men, becomes less significant than thinking more generally about the shaping of gender and how to become the person one wants to become.

The effect of this cultural shift on feminism is felt most keenly in discussion of the relationship between sex and gender. For second wave feminists, a clear distinction could be made between the two: 'sex' was relatively stable, set by the body; 'gender' described the cultural readings and shaping of bodily biological experiences. More recent configurations construct this relationship differently: *both* sex *and* gender are social constructions. Simone de Beauvoir, such an important figure for second wave feminism, argued in *The Second Sex* that 'one is not born, but rather one becomes, a woman' (1972 [1949], 295). Identity is shaped not merely by the body, but by cultural and social readings of it. If the sexed body retains its importance in Beauvoir's theorising, her identi-fication of 'becoming' shapes the work of later feminists (Hekman 2014). '"The body" is itself a construction,' Judith Butler writes at the beginning of her influential work, *Gender Trouble* (2006 [1990], 12). '*Woman* itself [sic] is a term in process, a becoming, a constructing that cannot rightfully be said to originate or to end' (2006 [1990], 45).

Initially, this claim seems empowering: it dislodges the constraints placed upon women as a result of their supposed nature. If 'Woman' is a distinct form of being, it is relatively easy to consign 'her' to a specific place in society, based on the supposed weaknesses of the female body. If, on the other hand, Woman is a *becoming*, there is a fluidity to identity that resists the imposition of restrictive stereotypes on the basis of rigid ontological claims.

There is much in the history of sexism that supports Butler's claims. Perceived ontological weaknesses of the female body have been used to justify claims for the inferiority of women in philosophies as different as those of Plato, Aristotle, Schopenhauer, Nietzsche and Sartre (Clack 1999). Sojourner Truth's use of her experience of physical labour to challenge those who would frame women as 'the second sex' is powerful precisely because she undercuts such claims from the lived reality of a body that is more than capable of the strength that is supposedly a feature of the male. But here is the rub. While Butler's emphasis on becoming offers a helpful way of resisting sexist stereotypes, what happens to the basis for a specifically feminist politics? If the sexed body does not provide a stable starting point for female identity, thus acting as a unifying sign for challenging stereotypes of the qualities of that body, what does it mean to be a feminist seeking the liberation of *women*? Is there a future for feminism in an age of becoming? Is there possible unity or only fragmentation?

This question becomes more pressing if we follow the direction of travel in Butler's theorising. Butler contends that *all* sex and gender identities are constructed. Beauvoir's social constructivist account of gender is reworked as 'performativity' (Butler 2014). Through the repetitive performance of socially constructed images of what it is to be male or female, we come to understand ourselves. Because identity is based upon performance, there is, however, the possibility of subverting these images: and the example Butler uses to show how this might be done is that of drag. Drag – the mimicking of femininity by males – offers 'a way of exemplifying how reality-effects can be plausibly produced through reiterated performances' (Butler in Armour and St Ville 2006, 282). Ideas of what it is to be male or female are subverted through playing with these ideas and challenging the notions of the body that lies beneath them. Butler has clarified the role of drag in her theorising on identity: 'It was never meant to be the primary example for gender subversion' (in Armour and St Ville 2006, 282). However, the ease with which it offers an image of the fluid gender identities she has in mind cannot be underestimated.

The feminisms taking their lead from Butler morph into more general studies of gender: *male* as well as female identity must be investigated. The aim is to explore the diverse expressions of desire and the myriad ways in which gender roles can be subverted and created. There may be a welcome fluidity to the construction of all forms of gender: we are not constrained by cultural accounts of how we should behave. Yet Butler acknowledges that there are limits to the work of identity formation: it always takes place in specific cultural settings and thus '*one does not set one's own terms of identifications*. One negotiates one's coming-to-be a subject in and through cultural norms regarding gender, sex, race, class and sexuality' (Armour 1999, 33; my emphasis). There are, it seems, limits to our imaginations. Acknowledging limits certainly challenges the utopian thinking that Lise Shapiro Sanders identifies as at the heart of feminist theorising. For Sanders, feminism needs 'the imaginative potential of utopian thinking' (2007: 6): we must dream dreams in order to imagine different futures and different societies. It may be, however, as important to think realistically about how we can change, perhaps transform, the material world of real political engagement.

Let us pursue the idea of limits as it shapes the politics emerging from Butler's gender theory. Butler's politics focuses on the possibilities of subversion rather than open resistance. This suggests a particular view of how to negotiate life in the world. Here is Butler: '*Subversion* was the preferred term because it communicates something of *the mire* [my emphasis] from which political agency emerges, and *resistance* tends to convey the purity and oppositional character of a stance' (Butler's 'Afterword' in Armour and St Ville 2006, 285). The idea of being 'mired' in a context or situation needs unpacking. The image is of being trapped, stuck in mud. Resistance requires a sense that this messiness can be escaped, and for Butler this seems to require a sense of the rightness of one's cause associated with forms of oppositional purity: *I* am right, *you* are wrong.

What to make of this image? Butler's approach suggests an unwillingness to accept the necessarily messy nature of attempts at resisting unjust relationships. But must political action be 'pure' in order to be undertaken? The realm of practical politics is forged by compromise and coalition and pragmatic fudge: necessarily so. To foreground 'subversion' as a form of political action suggests it is impossible to escape the context or stories that form the site for your oppression: you can only play with them. Martha Nussbaum's excoriating criticism of Butler focuses on this limitation. Consider slavery, Nussbaum says. Butler's politics suggests you can only subvert and play with your role; you cannot act against the institution of slavery itself (1999, 43). We might go further: a politics of resistance *requires* the power of the collective. An individual slave, playing with their image as slave, will never be strong enough to overcome the institution of slavery. Only forms of collective resistance will do.

A further question must be asked. Is identity only ever shaped by 'cultural norms'? *What of the body itself?* Is it mere malleable matter, bringing nothing of interest with it, nothing of importance for shaping life in the world? The physical body is strangely absent in Butler's theorising. Identity is located in my *reading* of my body: it is found in the *feelings* I have about how I want my identity to be. The questions informing the historical querying of 'Woman' take on new force. If (male) philosophers wanted to know 'Who is Woman?', now questions revolve around the extent to which bodily sexed identity offers a basis for identifying 'Woman'.[8]

---

[8] See Stock 2021 for current debates concerning sex and gender.

It is worth probing more deeply what is lost as well as gained with the shift to considering gender *and* sex as socially constructed and open to reconfiguration. The dangers of essentialism – that one's identity is grounded in a specific reading of the supposed 'facts' of physical existence – are obvious: women's biological role can all-too-easily be linked to claims of passivity and weakness, or to the natural world and animal life that 'rational, spiritual Man' attempts to avoid. Control over the female body can then be used to effect an illusion of control over nature (Ortner 1972). Yet downplaying the physical body for fear of falling into essentialist traps is not unproblematic. Claiming one form of lived experience common to all women may not be coherent if one accepts the diversity of experience; but that does not mean that the social conditions necessitating the emergence of the women's movement have disappeared. If 'Woman' can be defined as a political grouping arising *out of the conditions of female oppression* – Iris Young's contention (in Card 2010, 18–19) – what exactly are *the conditions* giving rise to female oppression? Investigating the social conditions that frame female embodiment, from cradle to grave, creates firmer ground for a revived feminist philosophy. It also opens up the importance of theorising life as something located in the body and its processes: vital for the feminist philosophy of religion advocated in Section 3.

1.4 A Feminist Politics of the Body

In 2019, Caroline Criado Perez published *Invisible Women*, an exposition of data bias in (as her subtitle puts it) 'a world designed for men'. If the feminism of the sixties and seventies focused on the struggles arising from female embodiment in a masculinist world, Perez's research reveals the detrimental affects on women of a context where assumptions of 'gender-neutrality' routinely employ the *male* body as the norm. Investigating everything from the design of cars that mean women are more likely to die in accidents than men (2019, 186–91), through the failure to diagnose heart attacks because listed symptoms apply to male not female physiognomy (2019, 217–20), to the inefficacy of drugs tested on the male body when taken by women (2019, 195–216), Perez shows that the body – its shape, its size, its processes – matters, and the disturbing reality of a context where 'the bodies, symptoms and diseases that affect half the world's population are being dismissed, disbelieved and ignored' (2019, 234).

Perez directs attention to the experiences of *the body itself* and highlights what happens to the *female* body in societies that continue to be configured around the life experiences of men. Claiming that physical sexual difference need not be taken seriously, for it, like gender, is constructed, is not without impact on the lives of women. The specificities of female embodiment – menstruation, conception, pregnancy, birthing, lactation, menopause – cannot be dismissed as merely contingent ways of reading the body. They impact upon the experiences of women, not least in the structures of the workplace, and this is particularly so when rendered invisible in the name of supposed gender-neutrality. Wishful thinking does not mean we cease to be physical beings. The body as a physical entity is far from irrelevant, and shapes much of what passes for the life experiences of women.

Butler's critique of Julia Kristeva's use of the maternal body suggests something of the form her response to such criticisms might take. Butler takes issue with Kristeva's suggestion of the maternal body as 'bearing a set of meanings that are prior to culture itself' (Butler 2006 [1990], 109). She rejects the claim that maternity is 'an essentially precultural reality' (Butler 2006 [1990], 109). Maternity, rather, is always shaped by cultural ideas of what motherhood involves. Certainly, stereotypes of motherhood have a long history in western thinking: so Marina Warner's classic study of the Virgin Mary (1990 [1976]) explores the history of Jesus' mother, while detailing the myths of maternity that emanate from her story. Yet to suggest the maternal body does not exist *apart from* such cultural overlays suggests a control over the reality of birthing and child-rearing that is not as possible as Butler (or we) might like. Butler's later reflections on loss and vulnerability (2006), in response to the 9/11 terrorist attack on New York, go someway to modifying this reading, but she remains hesitant about basing a 'universal' human condition on the body as an entity that can be understood outside its cultural formulations. Loss 'may have made a tenuous "we" of us all' (2006, 20), but that is as much as she is prepared to say about the realities of life that suggest we live 'at the will of the body' (Frank 2002 [1991]).

The range of experiences clustering around maternity suggest something of the problems with eschewing the physical conditions of female (and human) embodiment. Culture certainly shapes visions of the mother; but pregnancy is not simply a matter of feeling. Its physical reality reveals common ground between humans and animals: we, too, are brought into being, live for a time, and go out of being. The reality of pregnancy also highlights differences between male and female. At the very least, the bodily processes surrounding maternity point towards a shared female identity: an identity – a possibility – set apart from the identity and possibilities of the male body. For Butler, such claims are nonsensical: 'Is there a "physical" body prior to the perceptually perceived body? An impossible question to decide' (2006 [1990], 155). This dismissal of the physical body looks strange if approached through the experience of suffering: say, of the person with cancer, or the woman undergoing miscarriage or stillbirth. It is difficult to escape the conclusion that beneath Butler's philosophy is a form of Cartesianism that downplays the significance (and limits) of the body in favour of the possibilities of mind and consciousness. As Lise Nelson comments, 'the masterful subject' (1999, 332) haunts Butler's work, even as she attempts to challenge the autonomy of Enlightenment constructions of subjectivity.

The desire for control over the physical is easily understood. Maternity itself is not a state that is always easy to attain. For those who want to conceive but cannot, it confronts us with the limits of human will and desiring, not easily overcome by medical science. Evidence from the UK's Human Fertilisation and Embryology Authority suggests something of this fact: in 2018, birth rates per embryo transferred were 25 per cent for patients aged thirty-five to thirty-seven, 19 per cent for patients aged thirty-eight to thirty-nine, and 11 per cent for patients aged forty to forty-two. Patients aged forty-three and above consistently had birth rates below 5 per cent per embryo transferred when using their own eggs. Alongside these rather brutal figures is the knowledge that not all women can bring a child to term and that maternal death remains a reality. Life and birth does not always accompany conception; natality sits with mortality and death.

The self-actualising of Butler's account of identity rubs up against the constraints of the physical body. Echoes of the central tenets of neoliberalism can be heard in the hopes driving her project: you are an individual whose task is to 'stand out from the world', to create the life that you desire. Nothing lies outside human willing or choosing. The body is 'mute facticity', 'inert matter' (Butler 2006 [1990], 176); only of interest to the extent that it is shaped by human willing. With Foucault, Butler notes that 'the body is not a "being", but a variable boundary, a surface whose permeability is politically regulated, a signifying practice within a cultural field of gender hierarchy and compulsory heterosexuality' (2006 [1990], 189). Gendered bodies are 'styles of flesh' (2006 [1990], 190). Yet the realities of birthing, ageing, dying, challenge the extent to which such a reading can be maintained.

A further dimension gives us pause. Rendering the physical as valuable only when viewed as a manipulatable surface aggrandises the human at the expense of nature. An artificial distance is constructed between humans and the rest of the natural world. An alternative response is to accept the limits of human control: so Val Plumwood's ecofeminism (1993) resists ideas of nature as lifeless, only of value when acted upon by humans. Likewise, Patrice Haynes' account of the agency (activity) *and* 'patency' (passivity) of life entails attending to 'a life beyond the living, *a life irreducible to the terms of human agency* and the organism more generally' (Haynes 2014b, 143; my emphasis). We are *part of* – not *apart from* – the physical universe. A different ethics emerges from taking seriously the claim that we live at the will of the body: one which acknowledges *dependence on* – rather than *independence of* – the natural world.

Considering the realities of the lived body returns us to the *material conditions* shaping women's experience. Given the movement from industrial work to the service sector over the last forty years, it might be assumed that women will disproportionately benefit from the 'feminisation' of work. The skills associated with women – 'sociability, caring and, indeed, servicing' (Adkins 2002, 60) – seem more likely to be prized than skills associated with the male strength required in traditional manufacturing sectors. This has not proved the case: 'women's work' remains undervalued, and women in areas not ordinarily associated with female work continue to earn less than their male counterparts.[9]

In the world of work, theories of Woman meet the realities of life in a male-defined and dominated society. Combating structural inequalities that maintain the gender pay gap requires the consistent and persistent action that contributed to the formation of the trade union movement, women playing significant roles in trade union activities.[10] Emphasising the shaping of individual subjectivities does not sit easily with claims that lasting social change requires sustained, collective action. The philosophies shaped by Butler's ideas make 'coalition' the basis for feminist political action (Armour 1999, 183). Groups come together around specific issues, militate for change and then, when that change is attained, disperse. Moya Lloyd constructs a similar political agency that resists claims of 'natural' alliances based on class or sex identities. This 'reconfigured' politics renders the subject less a political actor and more 'a political effect' (Lloyd 2005, 6). Like Armour, Lloyd suggests a political realm where coalitions come into existence to address a specific problem before dissipating and dissolving. One wonders whether the trade union movement would have been as effective in addressing the needs of working people if it had followed such short-term strategies.

This may seem far from discussions in the philosophy of religion; yet lessons can be drawn from this political scene for a practical feminist philosophy of religion. If we start with the problem of inequality and the power of collective action, we might decide that a feminism is required that addresses real-world

---

[9] A survey by the American Association of University Women in 2013 showed women in full-time, year-round work earning 78% of their male co-workers. According to *Business Insider* (24 March 2015), only nine jobs saw women outperforming men in terms of pay. Women in the UK on average earn 87p for every pound earned by a man (see Daniel Thomas, Oli Eliot, and Dan Clark, 'UK gender pay gap widens despite pressure on business to improve', *Financial Times*, October 6 2021. Available from www.ft.com/content/239c95cc-d34f-43e9-a61e-faa7954277b6 [accessed 11 October 2021]).

[10] Three quarters of the membership of the largest UK trade union, Unison, are women. Unison's general secretary is Christina McAnea, the general secretary of the UK's Trades Union Congress, Frances O'Grady.

problems. Nussbaum sees in Butler's approach 'a dangerous quietism' with little to offer women 'who are hungry, illiterate, disenfranchised, beaten, raped' (1999, 43). A feminist philosophy of religion, concerned with developing an account of flourishing grounded in the ordinary practices of life, will, with her, take seriously these realities.

1.5 Feminism and the Philosophical Study of Religion: Liberating Praxis

Can today's feminism recapture something of its political force, while learning from the mistakes of the past? Can it do justice to the diversity of women's experience, while acting to utilise the collective power of women to oppose injustice and create a better society? I believe it can, but only if it ensures that the individualism of the last forty years does not become the final word on human identity. Taking seriously the human need for connection with the world and others provides promising ground for a feminism fit for the challenges of the twenty-first century.

The idea of connection provides a helpful starting point for feminist reflections on the religious. This framing requires shifting the gaze from generalised accounts of the spiritual to the communities that shape the religious life. If 'the spiritual' directs the gaze to the inner, private life of the individual, 'the religious' offers space for cultivating the depths accessible through enacting that internal gaze, while realising the importance of community for the flourishing human life.

1.5.1 The Spiritual Turn in Religion

Religious traditions present a host of problems for the feminist scholar of religion: not least because of the misogynistic past framing their practices and doctrines. Hampson's 'post-Christian' theology (1990; 2002) traces the roots of the problem to traditions that have at their heart the repetition of scriptures emerging from a patriarchal past. This historical grounding means no escape is possible from masculinist ideology, and thus Christian women should effect an exodus from organised religion, of the kind Mary Daly instigated at the end of her famous church service at Boston College in November 1971.[11] Considerable theological work is required to avoid such drastic actions: not least because of the foundation of Christianity in the acts of a male redeemer. For Hampson, it is easier to let go of the Christian God.

---

[11] Barbara Flanagan, 'Mary Daly leads exodus after historic sermon', in *The Heights*, Vol LXII, Number 11, 22 November 1971: https://newspapers.bc.edu/?a=d&d=bcheights19711122.2.4 Accessed 26 March 2020.

Christianity is not the only world faith encountering problems of the kind Hampson details. Susan Møller Okin directs attention to the role culture plays in shaping the practices of religious traditions: 'most cultures have as one of their principal aims the control of women by men' (Okin 1998, 667). The feminist scholar of religion ignores this history of male oppression at their peril. Any defence of multiculturalism cannot be at the expense of women's flourishing. Okin describes the problems of conservative forms of Judaism for women, along with her concerns about the veil in Islam. Such practices are ultimately based on understandings of the woman's body as 'an object of desire' (1998, 674), and Okin is not willing for this point to be passed over by those supporting a woman's right to wear it.

Okin's liberal feminism reflects her commitment to a set of universally applicable principles. She has a clear view of what it is to be liberated and what it is to be oppressed. As a result, she has been criticised by those who want feminism to reflect the diversity of women's experience. Jane Flax's critique identifies Okin's privileged whiteness. This factor leads her to be insufficiently careful in her understanding of the different ethical norms shaping different cultures (Flax 1995). Certainly Okin's critique is at its most convincing when she suggests the subtle psychological forms coercion takes in the private realm of the home: less so when read as a piece of embedded ethnographic research (Okin 1998, 676).

A more subtle analysis than either that of Okin or Flax is offered by Saba Mahmood. Mahmood considers the contemporary adoption of the veil as 'the means both of being and becoming a certain kind of a person' (2001, 215). Like Flax, she challenges the liberal feminist tendency to adopt an outsider perspective based on confident assertions of what the 'liberation' of women involves. But Mahmood's argument offers a more constructive way of proceeding than simply rejecting the concerns of liberal feminism: 'in order for us to be able to judge, in a morally and politically informed way, even those practices we consider objectionable, it is important to take into consideration the desires, motivations, commitments, and aspirations of the people to whom these practices are important' (2001, 225). Judgement is not suspended, simply placed in the context of listening to those who act in ways of which we might not necessarily approve. Greater understanding – if not acceptance – comes out of the active listening. Respectful conversation enables better relationships.

Mahmood's analysis critiques the liberal construction of agency. She uses aspects of Butler's politics of performativity to do this, but goes further, employing an ethnographic investigation of the lives of the women whose practices cause Okin's feminist consternation. Mahmood contends that her approach sits neatly with feminist claims that 'the personal is political': 'If there is one thing that the feminist tradition has made clear, questions of politics must be pursued at the level of the architecture of the self, the processes (social and technical) through which its constituent elements (instincts, desires, emotions, memory) are identified and given coherence' (2001, 224). While Mahmood accepts Butler's contention that 'one performs a certain number of operations on one's thoughts, body, conduct, and ways of being, in order to "attain a certain kind of state of happiness, purity, wisdom, perfection, or immortality",' she also considers the 'capacities and skills required to undertake particular kinds of acts', along, crucially, with 'the historically and culturally specific disciplines through which a subject is formed' (2001, 210). The account of agency that emerges is 'not as a synonym for resistance to relations of domination, but as *a capacity for action* that historically specific relations of subordination enable and create' (2001, 203; my emphasis). This approach, grounded in reflection on the life experiences of the communities she describes, makes the practice of liberation something more open than prescriptive judgements would allow. As she concludes: 'how would one imagine the politics of gender equality when situated within particular life worlds, rather than speak from a position of knowledge that already knows what the undoing of inequality would entail?' (2001, 224).

Mahmood's analysis gives a sense of the detailed work of the scholar of religion required by the feminist in order to avoid problems of over-generalisation and universalisation. Her concluding words alert us to the importance of context for understanding 'the particular worlds' inhabited by the religious. Feminist philosophers of religion, not necessarily trained in the work of the anthropologist or ethnographer, might prefer to direct their attention to broader investigations of 'the religious'. Rather than attend to the *practices* of religion – the rituals and rites, the communities that shape it – an alternative approach is to make what has been called 'the spiritual turn'. Here, attention is paid to the reflective life integral to the world's religions, rather than to the doctrines or practices of any specific religious tradition. While holding out creative possibilities, this is not unproblematic.

The shift to the spiritual defines some of the most important achievements of feminist religious imagination. As Melissa Raphael (1996) maps in her history of the 'thealogical' shift in feminist spirituality, figures like Carol Christ (1979; 2003) connect a spirituality of the Goddess with practices enabling the flourishing of the natural world. Anderson proposes a similar move from religious tradition to spiritual practice, albeit one shaped by a differing set of concerns. Anderson's article 'A thoughtful love of life' directs attention to the needs of a suffering world. Her feminist philosophy of religion is centred on fostering 'creativity for a world in need of a *love* of *life*' (2009, 125); yet her approach throws up (inadvertently) the problem of not engaging with 'the religious' in its concrete reality. In suggesting 'a spiritual turn' for the philosophy of religion (the subtitle for her paper), Anderson's focus, in line with her Kantian principles, is on the development of *individual* spiritual practice and reflection. The communal aspect of religion is left unmentioned and unexplored. While her conclusion claims that 'the other's response to one's own stories generates philosophy of religion as a philosophy of "that which binds us together" in a spiritual practice' (2009, 129), it is not clear what spaces Anderson envisions for this collective endeavour. It is doubtful that she means the churches, temples or mosques of the world's religious traditions, but something, instead, that arises out of a world that no longer accepts such Grand Narratives. Can the collective pursuit of that to which religion has pointed – that which lies outside the self, that is in the very fabric of the universe – survive the proposed turn to the spiritual?

Anderson is not alone in making the spiritual turn. Others, with Mahmood, find a useful conversation partner for this endeavour in Butler's theorising. Ellen Armour and Susan St Ville's edited collection *Bodily Citations* (2006) brings together diverse reflections by scholars of religion, united by the possibilities of Butler's performativity for constructing subversive forms of religious identity. What stands out in this collection is the hesitance about viewing actual religious communities as sites for resistance. If institutions are not present in the deliberations of the participants, neither is the body in its fleshy, messy reality. Language is the medium for constructing the body: without it, the body cannot be known. If this leaves something of a lacuna when it comes to thinking about physical reality, the editors seek to address this absence by utilising the 'trace' of the body, found 'in and through writing' (2006, xix). While neatly avoiding the dangers of biological essentialism, the result of this circumvention is an ethereal depiction of the human subject that lends itself to a distant and detached account of what religion involves.

Armour's 'Transing the Study of Religion' is a case in point. Drawing upon critical theorists Gilles Deleuze and Felix Guattari and their definition of 'materiality as constituted by change' (Armour 2018, 59), Armour describes all entities as existing in relationship, open to change and flux: 'There is no cosmic director or transcendental scheme according to which entities come into relationship with one another.' Some entities may persist (it is unclear which), but 'change, flux, newness and becoming' (2018, 59) are the principles directing Armour's shaping of 'religion's potential trans-formative role' (2018, 60). Religion 'has real material effects' (2018, 60); but note her emphasis is on 'effects' rather than the placing of such phenomena in specific contextual 'realities'. Armour's intention is to show how, by recognising the shifting, unstable nature of identity, it is possible to disrupt the boundaries between the ideas of religion and religious practice itself.

It is unclear, however, quite what transformative role this leaves for religion: and specifically how it relates to the lived experience of religious practitioners. Now, Armour is committed to locating her reflections in lived experience, as evidenced in her work on the failure to acknowledge race in white feminist philosophy. Yet there is something disconcerting about an account where the limits of physical beings are not addressed and where the focus is on the future shaping of subjectivity through the process of becoming.

This reified notion of transformation is troubling if we turn to the theme of Section 3: the problem of evil. Reflection on the problem of the suffering body suggests something of the dangers of a transformative account of subjectivity that pays insufficient attention to the realities of bodily identity. Hilary Mantel's *Wolf Hall* trilogy includes vivid descriptions of the burning of heretics. A particularly disturbing aspect of these torturous deaths is the way suffering undermines the very faith for which they are being executed. Here Mantel's protagonist, Thomas Cromwell, witnesses the execution of Father Forrest:

> When the heat reaches him Forrest draws up his blistered bare feet. He contorts himself, screaming, but is obliged to let his legs down into the fire . . . this stage seems to last a long time, the flames reaching upward, and the man's efforts to escape them ever more feeble, until at last he hangs and does not resist, and his upper body begins to burn. The friar raises his arms . . . as if he is clawing towards Heaven. The fibres of his body are shortened and shrivelling, his limbs contorting whether he will or no, so that what seems like an act of adoration to his papist God is only a sign that he is *in extremis*: and at a signal, the executioners step forward and with long iron poles reach into the flames, hook the roasting torso from its chain, and pitch it into the fire below. It goes with a scream from the spectators, a rush and spurt of flame; then we hear no more from Father Forrest. (2020, 555)

Such appalling torture silences the attempts of the sufferer to connect with their God. There is transformation here – a body turned to ash – but it is difficult to read this as a form of becoming. The body-in-pain directs the reader to loss as the shadow to the potential of transformation. The body is not simply a blank canvas on which cultural norms and individual desires are played out. What happens to the body affects identity and highlights the limits of shaping subjectivity howsoever we wish.

If the individualistic politics of neoliberalism and the new feminisms reflecting this cultural frame make it difficult to construct political forms of action aimed at resisting sexism, the turn to inner spirituality is similarly problematic for new religious formulations. Acknowledging the problems of patriarchal history for historical religious traditions alongside the power made possible by collective action, a different account of the religious can be offered: one that enables engagement with the sources of faith and that allows for a feminism more conducive to human flourishing.

1.5.2 (Re)Defining Religion

Armour's paper encourages us to think about what precisely religion involves. What does it *mean* to be religious? Is it primarily something private and individual, or does it hint at a broader collective identity, made real in religious community? Rather than think of religion in the abstract – either as a set of doctrines or through the lens of critical theory – I locate the religious in the *lived experience* of being human. There is something about human behaviour that is made manifest in the frameworks provided by religious traditions for how we might live in the world. The human animal might even be defined as *homo religiosus*.

This term appears throughout the history and philosophy of religion in a variety of ways (Bellah 1964; Hamilton 1965; Miller 1966): sometimes positively, as a means of denoting the desire for the sacred (Eliade 1959) or as a way of emphasising the importance of depth for the attempt to live well (Tillich 1965); sometimes negatively, to denote the tendency to false or super-stitious thinking (Barth 1934; Bonhoeffer 1971 [1953], 327). I use this term to reflect on the possibilities for a relationship with, and dependence upon, the world and others. This understanding of 'religious human being' enables a different feminist philosophy of religion than is offered by those who make 'the spiritual turn'.

Unpacking the term 'homo religiosus' reveals its usefulness for a feminist philosophy of religion. The Latin 'homo' resonates with the word 'humus' (earth): humans are 'earthly beings', literally, 'beings born from the earth'. Rather than attempting ways of 'standing out' from the world, humans are connected to the natural world, on which they depend for their existence. Neoliberalism and the feminisms springing from Butler's theorising suggest forms of identity unconstrained by the physical. *Homo religiosus* acknowledges limits, but also possibility. A disputed definition links the word 'religion' to the Latin 'religare', meaning, literally, 'to bind fast'. Religion involves the attempt to bind oneself or to connect oneself – to bind oneself *again* – to the world and others. Religious rites and practices, beliefs and ideas, can be read as attempts at *reconnecting* human beings to the world beyond themselves.

The religious attempt to *re*connect with the world suggests that the human animal is not entirely at home in their environment. The experience of consciousness – the ability to reflect on life in a mutable world – brings with it anxiety about human fragility in the face of natural forces that do not conform to human wishes. Heidegger suggests the 'homelessness' of the human condition (1983 [1947], 243); Freud makes the need to feel 'at home' in the world (Freud 1907; 1919) central to his account of the religious. If Freud links religion with superstitious ways of thinking, the connection he makes can be construed differently and more positively. The ritualistic practices of religion – worship, prayer, sacrifice – display the attempt to reach out to the world beyond the self. Humans are animals whose subjectivity is defined by relationship, formed out of our attempts at connection with others and the world.

The question of how such a being can flourish comes to the fore. For Jantzen, Arendt's concept of natality is crucial for shaping an account of the flourishing life and the ethic it requires. Arendt reorientates thought towards birth: humans are always capable of 'beginning something new' (1998 [1958], 135). Change is possible; death need not have the final word. There are echoes of Armour's transformative agenda in these words; the tone, however, is different. Reorientating the self towards natality makes relationship and community vital for shaping the human being. We are not 'thrown into the world', as Heidegger claims (Jantzen 1998, 149), for the ordinary facts of human existence show all to be born out of the female body, and thus into immediate relationship. A tangible physicality attends to this construction of community. The relationships into which the child is born are not perfect; indeed, serious thought is required to shape communities that enable the flourishing life. Hence the practical questions that shape Jantzen's philosophy of religion: How do we develop trustworthy community (Jantzen 1998, 204–26)? How do we live well (Jantzen 1998, 227–53)? How do we, to use her terminology, live in such a way that we are able to 'become divine'? My philosophy of religion builds on these questions: what principles and practices enable the truly flourishing human life for *homo religiosus*, the animal seeking connection? For Jantzen, part of the answer is in developing 'a holistic rather than the privatised, subjectivised spirituality' (1998, 170). This comment raises questions for advocates of the spiritual turn. How might we hold together the flourishing of the reflective inner life *and* the life lived with others?

By highlighting relationship, Jantzen challenges individualistic liberalism and its misleading universals. Is a feminist philosophy of religion possible that resists the reifying of choice denoting neoliberal political theory and individualist post-feminisms; one which directs the gaze, instead, to the lived experience of being in relationship, in community? The determination with which womanists direct attention to the communal nature of religion and the human subject provides a much-needed reorientation for feminist philosophy of religion. The lived practices of religious traditions become sources for enabling a changed perspective on the nature of the world and the place of humans within it. This perspective returns feminism to its roots as a political and practical movement. It is a way of thinking *and acting* that requires liberating forms of praxis that extend beyond the concerns of the self and towards a collective response to sex-based (and other forms of) injustice. Moreover, it demands a philosophical engagement with the practice of religion.

2 Community and the Flourishing Life: The Struggle for Truth

A significant point is reached in the attempt to reinvigorate feminist philosophy of religion. Understanding religion as shaped by the desire for connection, and placing this feature at the centre of feminist philosophy of religion, challenges overly individualistic framings of feminist aims: relationship and community are vital for and central to any account of what the flourishing life requires. This brings into sharp focus the need for practical solutions to the problems of living, a concern weaving its way through the framing of religion as a phenomenon reflecting the human need for connection. When Jantzen and Anderson make flourishing and love of life central to their feminist philosophising, they frame these notions, not as abstractions, but as practical concerns.

As Jantzen notes in her critique of analytic philosophy of religion (1996), we are beings shaped by time and place; thus a feminist project shaped in 2021 must pay attention to features of *this* time. Anderson and Jantzen's philosophies were necessarily shaped by the social trends of the late 1990s; chief amongst these, the self-confident individualism of neoliberal politics, then in its ascendency. The social democratic projects of Bill Clinton in the USA and Tony Blair in the UK tacitly accepted the global vision of neoliberal economics and the account of the individual stemming from it (Harvey 2005, 12–13).

An event casting its shadow over my feminist project is the Covid-19 Pandemic of 2020/2021. Far from being independent beings, defined in contra-distinction to the physical world, the pandemic has revealed our dependence on the will of the body, along with our connection to each other. Health is not something assured by the actions of the individual alone; it is ultimately only as good as the health of one's neighbour. The reality of dependence is also reflected in the growing demand that the ecological crisis be prioritised in our politics. That the global community will rise to this challenge is far from assured. The destabilising of 'facts' and 'truth' by populist politicians continues to shape the political scene of the early 2020s and makes concerted worldwide action to address climate change difficult, to say the least. Telling people what they *need* to hear – not least about the limits of the physical world – rather than what they *want* to hear does not easily attract support. Here, the unintended consequences of Anderson's and Jantzen's emphasis on the role of power in the creation of truth requires further thought. It may be that an account of truth transcending human desires and preferences *is* required in order to establish better ways of living with the earth.

With Jantzen and Anderson, I take seriously the location of the struggle for truth in communal life. While critical theory shapes much recent feminist philosophy, the insights of womanist and feminist theology offer the possibility of more complex engagements with the lived reality of community than is the case in more reified forms of philosophical discourse.

2.1 Investigating Truth in Feminist Philosophy of Religion

Given the significance of the investigation of truth-claims in philosophy of religion, it is not surprising to find that the projects of Anderson and Jantzen are concerned with questions of truth: what it is, and how, if at all, it might be established. The conclusions they reach reveal significant differences in their respective approaches.

Epistemology is central to Anderson's project. Creating a new society requires renewed grappling with how reality is understood. That this is a complicated task is made clear when Anderson turns a critical eye to the habitual practices – and practitioners – of the discipline. The apparent neutrality of philosophical accounts of rationality and objectivity, turned to the investigation of God, must be challenged, for the philosopher who is exercising rationality and arriving at 'objective' conclusions is not as neutral as might be supposed. Rather, they occupy a privileged place that is anything but classless or genderless (Anderson 1998, 36). Anderson has in her sights the maleness of the discipline: the lack of women practising it, the lack of key texts by women framing its content. The female is routinely excluded in a discipline whose neutrality is taken for granted through an uncritical acceptance of the texts *and men* framing its practice. Twenty years on, the maleness – along with the whiteness and Eurocentrism – of the foundational texts for the discipline remains contentious. Patrice Haynes' project to 'decolonise' the practices of philosophy of religion is 'not simply to expand the content of the philosophy of religion but to renegotiate the field altogether'.[12] Much work remains to be done to ensure an epistemological framework addressing the concerns flagged up by feminists of a discipline whose objectivity is anything but.

---

[12] See Haynes' project 'Animist humanism: decolonizing philosophy of religion in and through African cosmo-sense' at Stellenbosch Institute for Advanced Study. https://stias.ac.za/fellows/ projects/animist-humanism-decolonizing-philosophy-of-religion-in-and-through-african-cosmo-sense/

Anderson highlights the different responses feminists might make when confronted with the exclusions marring the work of the philosopher of religion. We might:

a) 'purge rationality of sexism';
b) 'seek less partial standpoints on rationality', taking seriously the material differences feminists expose;
c) see rationality itself as 'inherently male and patriarchal' (1998, 45), requiring subversion.

Anderson's solution is to turn to feminist standpoint epistemology; her aim, to provide a 'stronger' account of the objectivity on which truth depends. The account of truth that unfolds in this discourse is not partial, but based upon a complex view of objectivity that acknowledges the significance of perspective. Sandra Harding's work is central to Anderson's task, for it makes plain the difficulties involved in the quest for truth, and the necessity of paying attention to the multiplicity of perspectives that shape understanding of our world. According to Harding, 'feminist objectivity means quite simply socially situated knowledges' (Harding 1993, 64; in Anderson 1998, 74). Anderson clarifies this account of 'strong objectivity': it involves making space 'to think from the lives of others' (1998, 76); in particular, from 'the lives of marginalised others who include all women and some men' (1998, 84). Seeking to go beyond our limited perspectives enables an understanding of reality that is more complex and, as a result, more truthful.

While Anderson queries what passes for truth in philosophy of religion, she does not question the importance of critical reflection or the attempt to establish well-evidenced conclusions. Her later work, *Re-visioning Gender in Philosophy of Religion* (2012), makes this clear. Her method for philosophical reflection is explicitly ethical. The importance of truth is accepted, as a concept, but also as a way of living: 'If women and men today are to redeem *truth*, restore *faith* in *reason* and achieve change through *love* and *trust* in others, then we need to take a step back to reflect upon the concepts that currently direct our lives' (2012, 113). Her project is framed by Adrian Moore's claim that 'to possess a concept is to live by it' (in Anderson 2012, 114). Establishing the nature of truth requires the tools of philosophical reflection: a 'step back' is required in order to come to better understandings of life and how to live.

We noted the expansion of philosophical method defining Anderson's practice. Michèle Le Doeuff, the French feminist vital to Anderson's philosophy, rejects post-modern claims that 'rationality' is the problem. The real problem, Le Doeuff argues, is the exclusion of women from the practice of philosophy. She draws upon her experience of being told by a teacher that Kant's *Critique of*

Pure Reason would be 'much too hard for you' (Le Doeuff 2007 [1989], 144). This judgement on her abilities as a female student left its mark: she has never read Kant's text in its entirety, a response indicative of the ease with which women's self-confidence can be undermined. Fostering a sense of self *as philosopher* requires resisting the construction of philosophy along the lines of master/servant. Forget following a philosopher or school: instead, 'build up one's image as a philosopher' (Le Doeuff 2007 [1989], 151), for philosophical endeavour requires continual practice:

> Thought is thought about something: is this something properly understood? Does one's thinking reflect the current state of the problem? Does it show a sufficient level of information? Has it questioned itself enough? Is it accompanied by critical thinking? Does it open up new perspectives? (2007 [1989], 160)

Asking such questions is not to engage in arcane practices, but to make space for the creation of a more just world. Questioning one's experience is necessary to escape unjust situations, so critical thinking of the kind Le Doeuff outlines challenges the 'cognitive blockage' that renders the sufferer of domestic violence incapable of naming the reality of what is happening to her (2003, xv). Exercising rationality exposes the truth of a situation and makes possible the desire for justice.

Jantzen approaches the problem of patriarchally constructed reason differently, in a way that reflects Anderson's third possible response c): the construction of rationality requires subversion as it is 'inherently male and patriarchal'. Jantzen's attack is directed at the unacknowledged scientism of analytic philosophy of religion. The attempt to mirror the precision of 'science' in the philosophical investigation of religion is problematic, and Jantzen argues that 'the "scientific world-view" is itself a highly dubious grand narrative of modernity'. Its consequences for humanity and the planet are 'far more ambiguous than this determined hitching of religion to the scientific enterprise' suggests. Indeed, 'the methodology of western science . . . is responsible for many of the evils of modernity'. 'Science and religion between them have been patriarchal tools which have fostered racism, sexism and every kind of exploitation of people and the earth' (1998, 23). Given this damning appraisal of the model of neutrality and objectivity informing the task of analytic philosophy of religion, it is not surprising that Jantzen adopts a different approach: truth does not exist independently of human relationships. There is no 'reality' to be grasped outside the human shaping of it.

Jantzen turns to Foucault for her construction of what truth, in practice, involves: 'What counts as truth will be determined by those who have the power to do the counting' (1998, 193). As a result, she moves from the exploration of truth into an investigation of what is required for 'trustworthy' forms of community (1998, 204–26). Her focus is on establishing what allows for the nurturing of community, and what does not. A relational construction of trust drives her account, with 'trustworthiness' becoming a 'regulative principle' (1998, 212) for her philosophy of religion:

> Women (and men) holding themselves accountable for one another's flourishing, fostering each other as natals in the plurality of life, can in this shared commitment test the offerings of the imagination. (1998, 212)

She rejects attempts to 'justify true beliefs' in the philosophy of religion, arguing that the question of truth is 'an ethical and political question rather than primarily an ontological one' (1998, 212).

Jantzen's claims require revisiting. Jantzen stresses the significance of understanding historical context for shaping philosophical reflection; her approach, shaped by the optimistic individualism of the late 1990s, may not be as helpful as we might hope when viewed from the vantage point of the second decade of the twenty-first century.

The formulation of truth depends much on the times shaping the work of the philosopher. The themes determining the content of contemporary philosophising about religion are traceable to a web of sometimes contradictory concerns:

a) 'Faith seeking understanding' describes well the theological reflections of Anselm (1033/34–1109) and Augustine (354–430). They were not attempting to 'prove' God's existence; rather, philosophical analysis enabled deeper thinking about the nature of the God in whom they already believed.

b) The concern of Enlightenment thinkers – crucial for framing the method of the discipline – was to ensure that faith conformed to the dictates of reason. Kant's *Religion within the Boundaries of Reason Alone* (1793) provides a classic example of this approach: 'genuine' religion must be capable of rational shaping and align with moral principles.

c) If Kant's concerns inform contemporary philosophy of religion, the debates of twentieth century logical positivism have left their trace on the discipline. What is meaningful is that which can be aligned with scientific endeavour (Ayer 1971 [1936]). While logical positivist concerns are not explicit in today's practice, the desire to align religious belief with what can credibly be said in the face of scientific principles remains, as Jantzen suggests, a powerful lure.

The social context for *Jantzen's* approach reflects a comfortable and confident post-modernism. Under this methodological frame, the supposed correspondence of truth-claims with reality reflects the exercise of power. The feminist aim is to enable individual empowerment, and this effects Jantzen's proposals for philosophy of religion that cluster around attempts to 'enable women to achieve subjectivity' (1998, 20). She is critical of the extent to which assumptions about the centrality of belief to the investigation of religion can advance this. Truth is not outside the human, but something political; a conclusion that effects the way the flourishing life is to be established.

The world of 2021 rather undermines the optimism driving Jantzen's account. The rise of political movements that challenge the very notion of fact or truth have not been liberating for women or ethnic minorities. The regimes of Vladimir Putin in Russia (where opponents are routinely imprisoned and attacked), Jair Bolsonaro in Brazil (who rejects the reality of climate change) and Andrzej Duda in Poland (where women's access to legal abortion has been curtailed and where municipalities and regions declare themselves 'LGBT-free zones') are cases in point.

Making sense of the forces driving populist agendas is not easy, although the impact of the Internet and social media in 'democratising' access to information cannot be underestimated. This has not been an entirely positive development. Building on the erosion of faith in experts, the practice of *dezinformatsiya* ('disinformation') enables regimes to manipulate what passes for truth and thus remain in power.[13] As a result, opinions based on dubious forms of evidence – or just wishful thinking – proliferate across the political scene. The concise expressions of positions encouraged by social media platforms limits the possibility of detailed discussion, driving people into polarised positions, often expressed through the use of slogans: 'Make America Great Again'; 'Take Back Control'; 'Better Together'; 'Black Lives Matter'; 'All Lives Matter'; 'Transwomen are Women, Transmen are Men'; 'Woman Noun Adult Human Female'. I may agree with the intent behind some of these claims and the positions they espouse (indeed, a number of these examples reflect my views). Such statements may, when subjected to closer examination, reflect valid truth-claims. But making slogans the basis for one's politics can lead to the sense that detailed argument, respectful listening and informed debate is unnecessary and not to be encouraged. *I* am right and *you* are wrong: full stop.

Forms of political language that thrive on the adoption of slogans are not new, and the history of their use should give us pause. Writing at the end of 1942, Dietrich Bonhoeffer noted the role of slogans in shaping the political landscape

---

[13] See Kakutani 2018, chapter 8, for a guide to this phenomenon.

of his day. In a set of reflections 'on folly', written for his fellow conspirators against the Nazi regime, Bonhoeffer considered the way slogans encourage people to put aside their critical faculties. One's ability to think critically is given over to the 'charismatic' politician, who shapes what is then thought through the application of pithy catchphrases. It is impossible to have a proper conversation with someone who has given up their criticality: 'one feels . . . that one is dealing, not with the man himself, but with slogans, catchwords, and the like, which have taken hold of him' (Bonhoeffer 1971 [1953], 9). Shaped by the slogans of others, this person is 'under a spell, he is blinded, his very nature is being misused and exploited' (1971 [1953], 9). Abnegating the hard work of thinking for oneself has moral consequences. The person who does this is 'capable of any evil and at the same time incapable of seeing that it is evil' (1971 [1953], 9). We are far from the critical reflection Le Doeuff makes central to the work of (feminist) philosophy and the practice of liberation.

Arendt's report on the trial of Nazi war criminal Adolph Eichmann echoes Bonhoeffer's analysis. Eichmann does not present as a 'Master of Evil'; if anything, his defence suggests a man who has to fall back on cliches and catchphrases to explain his actions. The sheer banality of his language accompanies him even to the gallows: 'After a short while, gentlemen, we shall all meet again. Such is the fate of all men. Long live Germany, long live Argentina, long live Austria. I shall not forget them' (Arendt 1964, 252). Arendt identifies such language with the failure *to think*, something with grave consequences for Eichmann's ability to cultivate the empathetic imagination central to the quality of thoughtfulness: 'The more one listened to him, the more obvious it became that his inability to speak was closely connected with an inability to think, namely to think from the standpoint of somebody else' (1964, 49).

Elizabeth Minnich describes thoughtlessness as 'going on autopilot' (2017, 39). The erosion of critical thinking and the willingness – crucially – to open one's views up to challenge and discussion breaks the kind of open spaces Arendt makes central for healthy public discourse (Nixon 2015, 175). Passive acceptance of slogans ignores the hard work required to arrive at credible conclusions about any state of affairs. We become 'immersed in a fiction' (Stock 2021, 193) that does not allow space for critical thought. Jantzen's analysis of truth and power might, then, be framed as giving up too quickly on the necessary struggle for truth. As Harriet Harris notes, 'unless we are careful about belief . . . we can fall into, or fall subject to, bad or abusive practice' (2004, 75).

Arendt and Bonhoeffer's comments are framed by the events of the 1930s and 1940s; yet they sit comfortably with aspects of the current political scene. An interview with one-time Mayor of New York and legal advisor to President Trump, Rudy Giuliani, exemplifies something of the problem that accompanies the rejection of a truth existing independently of human desires and preferences. Asked why the White House was dragging its feet over arranging for Trump to be interviewed by Robert Mueller's investigation into Russian interference in the 2016 presidential election, Giuliani replied: 'When you tell me Trump should testify because he's going to tell the truth so he shouldn't worry, well, that's so silly, because it's somebody's version of the truth, not the truth' (Morin and Cohen 2018). Pressed on the logic of this contorted sentence – why should Trump have anything to fear if he told the truth? – Guiliani retorted, 'No, it isn't truth! Truth isn't truth.' For Guiliani, truth is never neutral: it is always shaped by the other's perspective and, crucially, their agenda. Michiko Kakutani, while accepting that post-modernist thinkers are not directly responsible for the rise of post-truth politics, criticises those who, like Jantzen, emphasise the subjectivity of truth (2018, chapter 2). Playing with forms of relativism enables unscrupulous political operators to challenge the possibility of any arena where 'the facts' might be made known.

This sortie into the quagmire of contemporary politics might seem a distraction from the work of the philosopher of religion. Tim Mawson describes philosophy of religion as a discipline 'loath to engage with ... empirical facts' (2005, 176). A similar unease is expressed by Yujin Nagasawa: if discussion of the problem of evil is shaped around its social manifestations, what exactly can philosophers of religion contribute, involved as they are in 'the rigorous analysis of religious beliefs and concepts' (2018, 139)? The methods of philosophy of religion are useful for clarifying the process of thinking and whether there are good grounds for the beliefs people hold, but it is not a discipline designed to engage directly with the lived narratives of political life.

Arguments like these underplay the possibilities of the critical distance enabling better understandings of reality for which Anderson and Le Doeuff argue. A relativistic philosophy has – no doubt inadvertently – contributed to a politics where everything can be reduced to opinion. Is it possible to accept the situated nature of knowledge *and* to align this epistemic position with the importance of striving for more truthful engagements with those amongst whom we live, and, indeed, with the world itself? Here is an important aspect of a practical feminist philosophy of religion: truth involves grappling with the consequences of the beliefs people hold, with argument and empirical evidence, just as it necessitates acting on the basis of those carefully thought out conclusions.

2.2 The Common Struggle for Truth in a Post-Truth Age

Jantzen and Anderson offer different responses to the question of truth in philosophy of religion. Anderson acknowledges that claims of objectivity have often been far from impartial, arguing for a renewed understanding of the importance of critical thinking. Acquiring stronger forms of objectivity is vital for her analysis. Jantzen emphasises the role of power in the construction of what is taken to be 'the truth'. The contested nature of what passes for truth leads to her alternative to Anderson's approach: one should choose 'a standpoint arising out of a chosen solidarity to make for flourishing' (Jantzen 1998, 212).

Anderson accepts that both she and Jantzen are concerned with transformation: the social world requires remaking, and, given the presence of sexism and racism, this involves struggle (Anderson 2012, 140). For Anderson, this means thinking about the concepts by which we live, and so she accept Miranda Fricker's comment that 'political beliefs are unintelligible in isolation from empirical claims about real states of affairs in the world' (Fricker 1994, 99; in Anderson 1998, 72). There has to be some correlation between what we claim, what we expose and what we hope to build. Truth is thus located in these practical activities.

Jantzen approaches the work of transformation differently. Rejecting concerns with attaining objective truth, she focuses on what is required to develop trust. Trust provides the glue for human relationships. Whether it is so easy to consign the concern with establishing the truth to the margins, given the realities of post-truth politics, is a moot point. The polarised positions attested to in the politics of the slogan turn the other person, not into someone with whom we might have a conversation, but into an enemy to be defeated at all costs. The sense of a shared public space is lost, and it is telling that President Joe Biden's acceptance speech in November 2020 sought to reject the polarised positions of the Trump era: 'We may be opponents but we are not enemies. We are Americans.'[14]

What does it mean to acknowledge this fraught context for political engagement? What is required if we are to live more truthfully? How do we establish communities based upon trust? Probing the relationship between truth and truthfulness offers a way forward. Bernard Williams – a key conversation partner for Anderson (2012, chapter 6) – connects the struggle for truth with two basic virtues: accuracy and sincerity (Williams 2002, 11). The notion of truth cannot be separated from the disposition of the one seeking it. At a time when deliberate falsehoods routinely masquerade as political reality (Oborne 2021), Williams' claim captures something important: the virtues of accuracy and sincerity act as guides in the struggle towards that which is true. As Williams puts it, 'you do the best you can to acquire true beliefs, and what you say reveals what you believe' (2002, 11). The struggle involved in the attempt to establish the truth cultivates character; the quest for it shapes our ability to live well in relation to those with whom we share our world.

---

[14] Joe Biden's acceptance speech, 7 November 2020 https://www.youtube.com/watch?v=1AfNYztas2c Accessed 11 October 2021.

The analysis of belief may not be as far from the creation of a flourishing space as Jantzen contends. In an important intervention, Harriet Harris considers what makes for healthy religious community. She rejects Jantzen's claim that little is gained for the flourishing community by engaging in critical reflection on belief. The example informing Harris' reflections emerges from the ramifications of the Anglican Church's attempt to hold together 'two integrities': those who accept the ordination of women and those who do not. Framed as a pragmatic solution to hold together a community, Harris details the uncomfortable reality of attempting to accommodate such radically different points of view. The woman attempting to fulfil her calling as priest can become disorientated by these tensions, undermined in her ministry to the point of feeling that she is going mad (2004, 80). The problem is not necessarily resolved by considering the sincerity with which different sets of beliefs are held: after all, those rejecting the priesthood of women doubtless believe what they say. What is required is critical assessment of the beliefs on which claims for a male-only priesthood are based. This is hard and difficult, and intensely practical: 'this is spiritual work, and involves wrestling with our community and wrestling with God, to allow truth to emerge' (2004, 81).

The attempt to establish the truth is not, then, a solely solitary task: it requires work *together*. Truth, and the attempt to attain it, cannot be separated from how one *lives* (the importance of cultivating the virtue of truthfulness). The possibilities for a practical philosophy of religion become evident. Beliefs, practices and traditions help shape one's thinking, affecting connection to the world beyond the self. The beliefs we hold matter; the question is whether they are worthy of being held or if they enshrine prejudices and uncritical opinions. As Harris notes, 'the struggle to expose partiality is a moral process with a moral goal, but does not on that count eclipse the concern for truth. Rather the attempt to articulate truth more fully is part and parcel of working toward greater goodness' (2004, 78).

Locating the struggle for truth in community informs womanist theologian Keri Day's reflections on Christian practice. Day notes that 'as Jesus is the truth, we must *be* the truth' (2016, 75). There is a *physicality* to truth; it is something to be lived out; and to establish the nature of that truth requires daily struggle. It is in the context of our relationship with others that truth is 'hammered out', as Patricia Hill Collins describes it, in words bringing to mind Nietzsche's exhortation to do philosophy with a hammer (Collins 1990, 15). As we engage with others, our beliefs are challenged, defended, fought for, given up and reshaped. This is so in the political and the religious realm.

Anderson's additional 'intellectual virtue' of 'reflective critical openness' (2012, 127) is crucial for this work, for it requires self-criticism. It is not enough to direct 'the suspecting glance' (O'Brien 2015 [1972]) at those holding different views from ourselves; a critical eye must be directed at the beliefs we *as feminists* hold. Are they justified? Why do we think as we do? What evidence have we acquired to support our claims? Is it good evidence? We are reminded of the questions shaping Le Doeuff's reflections on the on-going work of practical reason in the life of the philosopher.

A more complex engagement with truth thus opens up: and it need not lead to relativist conclusions. Collins highlights the importance of understanding ourselves as relational beings. The truth is pursued in community, whether or not this is acknowledged to be the case. Collins' focus is on the places where *black* thought is forged: in extended families, in schools where the community's children are taught, and within the black churches (Collins 1990, 15). 'The intellectual life' is not established in places that stand *apart from* the arenas in which everyday community is grounded. The truth is struggled for *in* community, and the truth that emerges is as necessarily complex as the lives whose perspectives it reflects.

To engage in the struggle for truth is to push at the boundaries of our experience. To take this seriously means acknowledging that much which currently passes for 'the truth' reflects the lives of a small number of those from the dominant classes. Our horizons must be expanded, encompassing and engaging with perspectives that open up further investigation of how the world 'really' is. The world we take for granted looks different when seen through the eyes of the the excluded and dispossessed; thus, attention must be paid to the way religious communities shape and support the lives of those whose worth is diminished in societies shaped implicitly or explicitly by claims of white supremacy. Religious communities offer the possibility of liberating space for those experiencing oppression. In a white supremacist society, the black church becomes the place 'where wounds are being healed and chains are being struck off' (Cone 1990, 134).

It is, of course, dangerous to romanticise the lived realities of community. Good community is not a given. Dialogue, challenge and resistance shape the daily struggle for truth. Womanist theologian Delores Williams describes this process as the 'terrible struggle for life and well-being' (1993, 203). To live truthfully, to commit ourselves to the virtues of accuracy and sincerity, to subject our own views to interrogation with as much energy as we bring to critiquing those of others, demands a continual renewal of the attitude that allows us to meet each other as human beings. Human society is messy, cultivating relationships hard and difficult. Replacing an abstract account of 'the individual' with an equally abstract vision of 'community' will not allow sufficient attention to be paid to the role of struggle in the making of *good* communities. Day's critique of neoliberalism combats the slide into romanticisation by offering a 'pragmatic politics of hope' (2016, 131). We meet each other as fallible human beings. Any unbending view of how to live is likely to break when confronted with the lives of different others. The challenge is to ensure that we grapple with beliefs and attitudes that cultivate dishonest relationships and undermine the ability to live well.

Delores Williams exposes this reality by considering the ambivalence of the black church for black women: the struggle to resist racism has not always been accompanied by a similar resistance to the evils of sexism. Rather than suggest women leave the church, Williams, instead, highlights the way in which 'black religion' has allowed for the psychological, emotional and physical security of black women (Williams 1993, 40; 46). The church as community is rarely simply good or bad, and just as Harris' critical response to the Anglican Church does not lead her to leave it, so Williams' work suggests the need to break the binary thinking that leads to simplistic accounts of what it is to live in community. The very support the black church lends to women is not without its dangers, as Williams highlights, and we might, with her, consider the often romanticised vision of woman as mother.

Grounding philosophical work in the realities of religious community gives added force to the careful, critical work Anderson makes central to her project. Locating that analysis in community demands reflection on the way ideas are expressed. Black liberation theologian James Cone dismisses the practices of 'clever' philosophy and theology as 'navel gazing', 'a luxury that oppressed persons cannot afford' (Cone 1990, 133). Likewise, Patricia Hill Collins begins her *Black Feminist Thought* with a statement of how she intends to write. Her voice will be 'both individual and collective, personal and political, one reflecting the intersection of my unique biography with the larger meaning of my historical times' (1990, xii). She criticises the use of theory that can be 'so abstract that it can be appreciated only by a select few' (1990, xii). Her aim, by way of contrast, is to present ideas 'in a way that made them not less powerful or rigorous but accessible' (1990, xii). Delores Williams, in tune with both, argues for a 'clear way of speaking' (in Cone 1990, 195). To express oneself other than in this way is to exclude those who might benefit from argument and critical thought. Clear language grounds philosophical reflection in the concrete experience of life in this world.

The demand for clarity to enable better forms of community does not sit comfortably with the technical language shaping much of the critical theory upon which contemporary feminist philosophy rests. Stock's suggestion for feminists is that they 'use less academic (high) theory, more academic data' (2021, 271) in furthering their politics, and the same might be said of the approach to be taken by the feminist philosopher of religion. Truth matters if the flourishing community is to be built; it should reflect the lived reality of human relationships; and it must be expressed in ways that enable all women to gain from it. Anderson cites bell hooks with approval, in words that make central truth-telling, while opening up the problem of lies and deceit:

> To make community, we need to be able to know truth, to speak openly and honestly. Truth-telling has to be a spiritual practice for many of us because we live and work in settings where falseness is rewarded, where lies are the norm. Deceit and betrayal destroy the possibility of community. (in Anderson 2012, 125)

Locating truth in the practices of community does not gloss over the reality of lies that break the possibility of flourishing communities: if anything, identifying lies and challenging them takes on new importance for this practical work. This grounded approach to truth opens up reflections on the problem of evil – such a key topic in philosophy of religion – in surprising ways that lead towards practices enabling the flourishing life.

3 God, Lies and the Problem of Evil

3.1 Groundwork for a Feminist Approach to the Problem of Evil

Does a feminist ethic *require* an investigation of evil? To use the word 'evil' suggests a metaphysical distinction between what is Good (or 'God') and what is Evil (or 'not-God'). It does not sound particularly promising for a *practical* feminist philosophy of religion to direct attention away from the human realm to some hypothetical otherworld where a battle is being waged between absolute cosmic forces. For Mary Midgley, focusing on human behaviour offers a better way of proceeding, for regardless of whether or not God exists, no one can escape the manifestations of evil (1984, 1–2). Midgley's words direct attention to how wickedness arises in human life and the need to combat it. The feminist philosopher of religion might well agree with such an approach.

There are, however, good reasons for employing the language of evil, and a number of arguments are helpful for the feminist philosophical project I advocate. At times, only the word 'evil' is sufficient for grasping the terrible extent of human cruelty. Marilyn McCord Adams gets at this well with an extensive list of examples of what she designates as 'evil'. These actions and events challenge easy theological answers, and in highlighting this aspect she shares common ground with Eleanor Stump's attempt (2010) to ensure analytic philosophy of religion engages with the full horror of evil. 'Evil' is the only word with sufficient force to describe events where no positive value whatsoever can be accrued *by the sufferer*, and McCord Adams makes painfully clear the experiences she has in mind: 'the rape of a woman and axing off of her arms, psycho-physical torture whose ultimate aim is the disintegration of personality, betrayal of one's deepest loyalties, child abuse of the sort described by Ivan Karamazov, child pornography, parental incest, slow death by starvation, the explosion of nuclear bombs over populated areas' (1999, 26).

McCord Adams does not shape an explicitly feminist philosophy: Claudia Card does in her reflections on evil. Like McCord Adams, Card addresses the horror of evil, and her 'atrocity paradigm' (2005) reveals common ground between the two positions. This is evident when she claims the necessity of using the language of evil. Card identifies 'evils' with 'inexcusable wrongs': note the plural. This is not about identifying some force *outside* human life and action. Rather, this word describes actions that challenge the ability to comprehend them: 'Evils are reasonably foreseeable harms produced (maintained, supported, tolerated, and so on) *by culpable wrong doing*' (2010, 5; my emphasis). With McCord Adams, Card's focus is moral evil, for this is where the 'real' problem of evil is located (I address 'natural' evil in Section 3.3). Two components are vital for Card's identification of evil: 'harm' and 'agency'. It is *deeds* and *practices*, not attempts to put 'labels on people (or empires or alliances)' (2010, 5), that must be central to the discussion. 'In atrocities the ingredients of evil are writ boldly' (2010, 6), Card says; and this means that 'evil on the atrocity paradigm wears a human face' (2010, 16).

Card's practical focus alerts us to a feature common to feminist approaches to evil and suffering. If analytic philosophers of religion fall back on a construction of the problem of evil as a puzzle that requires solving – so, 'how is the Omnigod of theism to be held alongside the reality of evil and suffering?' – the feminist focus is on the phenomenon itself and its grounding in forms of human behaviour and social structures. At the same time, attention is paid to evils not ordinarily considered by philosophers of religion. Thus, Card emphasises evils visited overwhelmingly on the female body. How she does this is insightful, for it suggests the connection between the individual and the social that informs feminist analysis. Card details the experience of 'rape terrorism' (2010, 159), an atmosphere that creates a context of fear for *all* women, regardless of age, ethnicity or economic class. Susan Griffin's classic essay on this phenomenon, 'Rape: An All-American Crime' (1971), illustrates Card's point:

> I have never been free of the fear of rape. From an early age I, like most women, have thought of rape as part of my natural environment – something to be feared and prayed against like fire or lightning. I never asked why men

raped; I simply thought it one of the many mysteries of human nature. (in Card 2010, 160)

Rape is not 'merely' a personal experience; it is a method that perpetuates the system of patriarchy. The reality of rape shores up male political power by rendering women fearful and powerless. Rape is thus socially constructed. Card's reading is supported by her analysis of rape as a weapon of war. The female body, its abuse and ownership, becomes the arena on which male desires for political power are played out. Card's example is from the Bosnian war of the 1990s where rape was routinely employed as a means of terrifying and demoralising one's enemies, as well as creating ethnic homogeneity.[15] Card's argument builds on the second wave analysis of sexual violence and makes its identification and resistance to it a central part of feminist activism. Rape is personal *and* political.

Card's atrocity paradigm is not without its critics, and these criticisms direct us to a strand in the feminist engagement with evil of importance for my practical philosophy of religion. Samantha Brennan argues that Card's focus ignores the connection between atrocities and what she calls 'everyday inequalities' (Brennan 2009, 141). Brennan's examples seem small-scale compared to the horrors of terrorism, torture and genocide peppering Card's analysis and providing plentiful (disturbing) examples of how harm and agency unite to create all-too-human evils. Brennan's gaze, by way of contrast, is directed to the personal and the private.

Brennan addresses the link between domestic violence (which in its most extreme forms provides examples of the horrors Card details, and which is also overwhelmingly inflicted upon women) and low pay (an everyday inequality that, again, disproportionately affects women). Identifying a connection between two such different phenomena might seem strange. Yet for Brennan ordinary inequalities, such as limited independent financial resources, are often a significant factor in limiting a woman's ability to escape her abuser. Brennan provides empirical evidence from Rhona Mahony's study *Kidding Ourselves: Breadwinning, Babies and Bargaining Power* (1995): 'A woman who has a higher income can walk out on a violent man more easily. Or she can credibly threaten that she'll walk out' (in Brennan 2009, 154).

Brennan is convinced by Mahony's claim: others might wonder whether purely economic factors capture the whole story. The psychology of dependence and coercive control suggests a more complex reality, as is illustrated in the

---

[15] This is far from a purely historic example: see Matthew Hill, David Campanale and Joel Gunter, '"Their goal is to destroy everyone": Uighur camp detainees allege systematic rape.' BBC News 2 February 2021, www.bbc.co.uk/news/world-asia-china-55794071.

case of Sally Challen, convicted for murdering her husband in 2011. Challen's conviction was converted to manslaughter at appeal in 2019. Clare Wade QC, conducting Challen's defence, drew attention to the various forms of 'coercive control' used by Challen's husband for over thirty years. Coercive control is 'bespoke abuse' 'in the sense that the perpetrator will tailor the control to his victim's specific vulnerabilities': so, 'isolating her, cutting off finances, monitoring her movements, micro-regulating domestic duties and so forth'. Economic resources are part of the context that makes leaving impossible, but so is the assault on agency and the networks that would make leaving possible. As Wade says in her reflections on the case, 'the court should approach domestic abuse from a perspective of *social and personal* entrapment' (Wade 2020; my emphasis). Brennan's more general point comes to the fore: Card's attention to atrocity runs the risk of ignoring ordinary social phenomena – limiting independent finances, undermining confidence, creating a sense of isolation – that allow evil to flourish.

Brennan's criticisms and her understanding of the nature of evil resonate with Hannah Arendt's description of the 'banality' – the ordinariness – of evil. At Eichmann's trial, Arendt is puzzled by how little he looks like the popular image of a war criminal. He presents as an administrator or a librarian, not a figure of evil. Both claims are, in fact, true: Eichmann was the chief administrator of the transportation system that took the Nazis' victims to the death camps. This meshing of the ordinary with the extraordinary is what makes Eichmann so troubling. For Arendt, he is a 'new type of criminal' (1964: 276); one whose crimes emerge from a particular set of social conditions and working practices. Arendt, like Brennan, directs attention at the social context that enables the creation of such a person.

Arendt emphasises institutional practices that created Eichmann and those like him. Dependence on bureaucratic systems for structuring the state and shaping human behaviour (Arendt 1968 [1948]) lead to the fragmentation of tasks and the focus on achieving a set of predetermined end results. Employed in such systems, individuals are rendered incapable of associating *their* specific tasks with the broader agenda of their employers. There may be good reasons for instigating systems of this kind: the efficiency of 'the System' appears preferable to reliance on the messy idiosyncrasies of fallible individuals. Yet Arendt argues that disparaging human relationships creates a problem far greater than the one the System is supposed to solve. The worker, conceived as 'a mere function' of the organisation (1968 [1948], 215), becomes 'aloof' from the ordinary human concerns that would enable them to identify the effect of their actions on the lives of others. The very precision and efficiency of the bureaucratic system obscures the reality of a common world shared with others, and it is this shared world that Arendt urges us to reclaim:

In comparison [to bureaucratic societies], exploitation, oppression, or corruption look like safeguards of human dignity, because exploiter and exploited, oppressor and oppressed, corruptor and corrupted, still live in the same world, share the same goals, fight each other for the possession of the same things; and it is this *tertium comparationis* which aloofness destroyed. (Arendt 1968 [1948], 212)

Eichmann is disturbing because he is not a 'monster' detached from the rest of humanity: the conditions that created him fostered countless others without whom the Holocaust could not have happened. These conditions did not end with the liberation of the death camps and the end of the Second World War, for *they are replicated every day in the institutions and practices of daily life*. When Elizabeth Minnich offers her contemporary reworking of Arendt, it is the everyday that drives her analysis, distilled into a very ordinary question: 'what were they thinking?' (2017, 1–4). It is not so much that creating Eichmanns who attend only to their task in an organisation necessarily *leads to* the horrors of the Third Reich; rather, it is the construction of one's daily activities in this way that should make us pause, for it does not take much for the dulling of critical moral thinking to be used by those wishing to do harm.

Minnich's examples are derived from a succession of extensive, systematic evils; her concern is with the comparatively small actions and attitudes enabling such events. Consider the phrases shaping the actions of those engaging in genocide that are mirrored in the daily practices of societies not engaging in such horrors: 'Don't take it home with you … Be a team player … It's not our business; I was just doing my job; everyone else seemed okay with it; who was I to question the guys in the big offices? I had a family to support. There was a promotion I could get if I played it right' (Minnich 2017, 12). Ordinary concerns with self-advancement become anything but when used to explain one's failure to challenge genocidal agendas: 'the killing was a job, not a vendetta; it was nothing personal; working hours pretty well contained it. The killers could sleep well, and, next day, continue their work' (Minnich 2017, 1). Wilful blindness to the effects of one's actions is an important condition for evil.

The connection between the everyday and atrocity is more complex than might initially be thought. Attitudes seemingly irrelevant to acts of genocide cultivate ways of thinking that dull the moral senses and, if the circumstances are right, can be used by the perpetrators of such actions to their pernicious ends. As Arendt says of Eichmann, he 'commits his crimes under circumstances that make it well-nigh impossible for him to know or to feel that he is doing wrong' (1964, 276). *Thoughtlessness* – the failure to engage in empathetic and critical thought – provides fertile ground for evil to flourish. The solution to the problem of evil, Arendt and Minnich claim, requires the cultivation of *thoughtfulness*.

Arendt's analysis offers much to feminist and womanist analysis of social structures supporting oppression and violence (Welch 1989; Townes 2006). Evil is not so much a force transcending the actions of human beings as something relational, located in social structures and personal relationships. 'Evil occurs between people' (Geddes 2003, 105), as Jennifer Geddes claims in words that also permeate Minnich's analysis.

Against the backdrop of a relational account of evil, lying emerges as an important theme for feminist analysis. As bell hooks indicated at the end of Section 2, the practice of truth-telling is vital for creating the conditions for trust upon which flourishing communities depend. What we say matters, and societies where the lives of others are misrepresented by lies and falsehoods are open to everyday (and extraordinary) forms of injustice. The Holocaust depended on the lies of antisemitism that stretched back centuries; the slave trade on economically driven lies that rendered black people less than human. For feminists, attention must be paid to the social impact of lies told about women.

It can be a surprise to encounter claims that women are responsible for evil (Noddings 1989, 35). In Greek and Roman myth, the first woman, Pandora, was the source of all human suffering. Described as 'the calamity for men who live by bread' (Hesiod 1988, 39), Pandora foolishly opens the box containing all the misery of the human condition. In the Christian tradition, suffering is similarly traced to the first woman. Eve's failure to resist Satan's temptation leads to the expulsion of humans from Eden, while opening the door to the punishment of death. Such stories reflect attitudes towards women common in the times that created them, and inform later theological and social misogyny (Pagels 1989). Evil enters the world through a woman, and all women, as 'daughters of Eve', are, at worst, incapable of goodness, and, at best, limited in their ability to pursue the moral life. Without the 'weakness of woman', there would be no evil, for the devil would never have dared approach the stronger Adam (Tertullian, in Clack 1999: 50). Woman's responsibility for evil is located in her very being, and thus social constraints on women's lives are required to curb her excesses. Woman is incapable and dangerous, and requires treating as such.

So much for the refrain against the fallible female encountered in Section 1. An added dimension should be noted. Beneath the words of female culpability for a broken world is an equally troubling account of nature. The gendered division between nature and reason is replicated in the split between the world and humanity. The role of the male is to control the fallible female; the role of the human is to dominate unruly nature. Practical questions of how to live well in the world cannot escape discussion of truth, lies and evil. Here, the philosopher of religion finds themself on familiar ground, for questions about God and the truthful depiction of reality are central to the ethical life.

3.2 Rethinking God and the Ethical Life

Considered against the backdrop of these reflections on evil, the principles of accuracy and sincerity from Bernard Williams, Le Doeuff's critical thinking and Anderson's reflective critical openness become, not mere philosophical abstractions, but vital starting points for the practical work necessary for creating flourishing communities. If we do not attempt to make our language reflect reality, if our words mask our own agendas, if we are not sufficiently reflective and honest, we will not enable the conditions necessary for the flourishing not just of ourselves, but of others, and, moreover, the world itself.

Are these principles enough to create the flourishing life that is the aim and hope of feminist philosophy of religion? Nietzsche offers a rather more challenging rendition of the struggle for truth than has been encountered so far. He accepts (in an echo of Jantzen's claims) that values are not politically neutral: 'the truth' – as it is presented by individuals and in communities – is not something detached from relationship. There is indeed (as Collins says) a struggle for truth; but Nietzsche's model for this reflects a hierarchy of relations where the differing desires of 'masters' and 'slaves' inevitably come into violent conflict. The truth is determined by whoever emerges from the fray victorious; so, yes, it is not fixed: it is open to change. Thus, the 'transvaluation of values' is the project for Nietzsche's 'Ubermensch', who comes after humanity and who is prepared to realise the consequences of the death of God (Nietzsche 1998 [1886], Section Two; 1969 [1883–85], Part One). Nietzsche's thoughts make for uncomfortable reading, and, while it is certainly not necessary to accept his as the only model for the struggle for truth, his words challenge any cosy account of what this involves in practice. Given what John Roth calls the 'slaughter bench' of human history (1981, 10), it is perfectly plausible to ask whether humans, understood as entirely self-creating, are sufficient to the task of creating societies that are good for all, rather than just an elite few.

Simone Weil (1952) explores this problem when she considers the advocacy of human rights in the wake of the horrors of the Second World War. It is worth the feminist reflecting on her words, for they certainly dispel easy grounds for optimism. The language of rights, Weil argues, while laudable, is not particularly helpful for enshrining respect for the lives of others. Rights can be challenged, changed, ignored: all is dependent on the context in which we find ourselves. Instead, she advocates the *impersonal* recognition of 'the human' as the frame for our values. Rather than rights, she foregrounds the *obligation* to meet the *needs* of others. Out of the construction of obligation and need emerges an ethic of the flourishing life that requires human beings to consider their duties to each other as beings demanding attention. For Weil, the web of needs and obligations is more fundamental than the more artificial overlay of 'rights'. Moreover, her model for human relationships is grounded in the creative action of God. The 'attention' to each other that is central to Weil's ethics is love, for it is 'God in us who loves them' (1959, 107). She does not ignore the importance of human relationship and community, but these cannot stand alone. Instead, the basis of these relationships is in something transcending the preferences and desires of individuals. Only in this way can the value of each individual be secured, and this requires a shift in the understanding of God: 'we must conceive of God as impersonal, in the sense that he is the divine model of a person who passes beyond the self by renunciation' (1959, 133).

Weil's ethical concerns open up the question of the character of the God who acts as guarantor for the ethical life. To explore the significance of her claim requires revisiting some arguments I presented in previous work on the problem of evil. Then, I argued that a practical feminist philosophy of religion need not address the traditional arguments that attend to the co-existence of God and evil, for the urgency of the problem of evil is felt, 'not in the attempt to justify the ways of God to humans, but in the way it forces reflection on the conditions and attitudes that hinder human flourishing' (Clack 2018, 135). I have come to revise that view. It *is* necessary to include discussion of the importance of God, religion and the divine for shaping the well-lived life, for the reasons that Weil identifies. Questions that are *existential* because they turn the gaze to the nature of existence, and *theological* and *ontological* as they require us to think about the nature of reality itself, are not easily separated from ethical questions of how to live.

The accounts of evil considered so far effectively park theodical arguments in favour of practical measures that challenge moral evil. Arguments surrounding God appear as distractions from this task grounded in reality. Sure, Arendt reports that Eichmann 'feels guilty before God, but not before the law' (1964, 21), but she does not discuss what Eichmann intends by using this phrase. Instead, her discussion moves onto questions of jurisprudence: does the court in Jerusalem have the authority to try Eichmann for crimes committed outside its jurisdiction? Yes, Card uses the language of evil; but rather than muddy the waters with theological concepts, she proposes a 'secular understanding of evils' (2010, 4).

A practically focused feminist philosophy of religion will find much to approve in reconfiguring the problem thus. A philosophy concerned with the attempt to live well will look to catalogue, challenge and *change* the conditions leading to the tortures and injustices Card *et al* highlight. However, excluding discussion of God neglects an important aspect of the investigation of the conditions that allow for evil, while limiting discussion of what exactly is meant by 'the good': that aspect of life so relevant for the feminist concern with flourishing. Minnich makes discussion of the 'ordinariness of the good' the companion theme to the banality of evil, and in doing so she brings the religious life into sharp focus, while opening up space for discussion of what, precisely, is meant by God or the Divine.

Minnich explores Philip Hallie's (1979) investigation of the village of Le Chambon and the role that daily religious practice played in framing that community's hospitality to Jews fleeing Nazi persecution. Hers is a secular study, yet Minnich notes 'that religion plays an important role in this story' (2017, 120): those offering the hand of friendship to the persecuted were members of a Huguenot religious community. While religious practice is central to this case, Minnich is not convinced that this is necessary for cultivating the well-lived life. Religious people, after all, are just as capable of unthinking wickedness as anyone else.

Grist to Minnich's mill is provided by the observations of Le Chambon's Pastor Andre Trocme and his wife Magda Grilli Trocme on why they and their fellow villagers acted as they did. They speak 'largely in secular terms' out of 'the profound conviction that whatever your religion, it is *how you choose to act with and for others daily, in ordinary life and when the ordinary has been perverted*, that matters' (Minnich 2017, 120; my emphasis). The practices of kindness to the stranger or outsider, enshrined in peace time, meant that when the villagers were faced with refugees fleeing persecution they held out the hand of friendship and hid them from their persecutors. This was not about 'heroism', but about responding to the needs of the stranger. 'It had to be done, that's all', was Magda Grilli Trocme's rather dismissive response to those seeking to frame their practical humanity as an act of extraordinary goodness (in Minnich 2017, 122).

There may be no easy correlation between religious belief and ethical action, yet this example of 'extensive goodness' (Minnich 2017, 124) casts light on the practical possibilities of religious faith. Cultivating daily practices, developing a mindset of compassion towards others through religious practices that ground faith in the love of God and of neighbour, shaped the life of this little community, and made possible – provided the ground for – their acts of heroism. The philosopher of religion might usefully probe the question of *which* concepts of God best nurture this kind of ethical faith. This task is rather different from that arising from discussion of the qualities of the OmniGod. When God is defined as an agent with a particular set of characteristics, ethical questions get caught up in the attempt to explain the presence of evil and suffering in the world 'He' created. The God who is 'like us only greater' emerges from such discussions as a rather inept cosmic architect, the world 'He' created scarce fit to live in (see Hume 1998 [1779]: Part X). But adjust the meaning of the word 'God' towards something more radically non-human and impersonal in the way Weil suggests – say, to Melissa Raphael's Shekinah, 'the female face of God' who hides that face in Auschwitz, but is 'still there, because there is no place where she is not' (2003, 154); or Richard Rohr's 'another word for everything' (2018, 34); or Paul Tillich's 'the God above God' (1977 [1952], 180) – and the discussion develops quite differently. Questions concerning God and evil become less about solving an 'inconsistent triad' (Mackie 1955), and more about how to respond to the challenges of life. Holocaust survivor Viktor Frankl makes explicit this ethical framing. We are 'questioned by life' (2004, 85) when the things that happen to us and those we love force us to address what exactly we live by. This is a much more useful way of proceeding than thinking of 'the problem' of evil, for it is a task that none can escape, regardless of the religious positions held. All of us have to find ways of living with the things that happen.

Yet the question of 'God' remains. Let us return to Weil's contention that only a *transcendent perspective* enables a firm foundation for the ethical life. Dancing as she does on the boundary between Christianity and Judaism, her thought resists attempts to pin down too rigidly the language of the divine. Using theological language, however, is almost inevitable if we are to follow her lead and think seriously about what makes for an adequate grounding for the well-lived life. While the philosopher of religion may feel a sense of relief as the question of God returns to the discussion, the focus that emerges out of feminist reflection on the practice evil is different: the concern is now with rejecting models of the divine that do not take seriously the reality of evil and suffering, while identifying those that enable the flourishing life.

The OmniGod seems less than helpful for this ethical endeavour. The attributes of omnipotence, omniscience and perfect goodness do not easily survive an acceptance of evil and suffering as features of this world. Either the crushing reality of evil and suffering has to be diminished – so, 'it is a necessary part of God's plan for human beings' – or one of the divine attributes has to be modified or removed. God is either not all-powerful (so the suffering God of Moltmann (1973), Soelle (1975) and Bonhoeffer (1971 [1953]); or God is not all-loving (Roth's (1981) terrifying God, responsible for the bloody history of the world).

Jantzen's solution is to shift the discussion of God into the realm of individual subject formation. In so doing, she builds upon Irigaray's claim that men have always had a model of the divine that enables the development of their masculinity. Consciously or not, the availability of male models for God has provided men with a transcendent perspective – a template, if you will – for the work of identity formation. Women, Irigaray argues, lack a divine horizon that aids the creation of *their* distinctive subjectivity. Acknowledging this lacuna goes beyond discussion of the limitations of holding to the male generic in theological language. In the context of female self-creation, the 'maleness of God' does real harm. Women cannot without difficulty apply masculine theological language to their understanding of themselves, and thus are forced, if they remain within the Abrahamic faiths, to contorted forms of self-understanding (Jantzen 1998, chapter 2).

Jantzen's solution is not to follow Carol Christ (1979) in replacing the male 'God' with the female 'Goddess'. Instead, Jantzen's focus is on the activity of 'becoming' (1998, 257). By moving towards a divine horizon, there is the possibility of transformation: and the divine is located in this '*process* of becoming' (1998, 255). This solution resonates with the language of feminists who would employ Butler's philosophy of gender to reshape the work of religion.

Jantzen's understanding of 'God' is shaped by the notion of a divine horizon towards which we move as we create the self. There is a form of transcendence here, but it is a '*sensible* transcendent' (1998, 266; my emphasis). This phrase reflects the role of pantheism in Jantzen's earlier philosophy of religion (Jantzen 1984). The transcendent is grounded in the immanent, and a phrase from Irigaray gives a tangible sense of what Jantzen has in mind: in our becoming, we are 'bringing the god to life through us' (1998, 272). 'God'/the divine is located in the activity of human becoming. Denying the binary construction of 'transcendence' as opposed to 'immanence' makes plain, she contends, our obligations to this fragile world. She has little patience for those who would make of their 'desire for a "better world"' (1998, 147) an enemy of *this* world. *This* is the world we have, and each life in it 'special ... to be affirmed and celebrated' (1998, 148). This has practical implications for the work of flourishing: if the divine is becoming, so 'becoming divine is inseparable from solidarity with human suffering' (1998, 263). Political action emanates from this embodied notion of the divine, while also highlighting Jantzen's framing of the problem of evil.

At this point, Weil's questions reemerge in ways that reflect my own preoccupations. In collapsing the transcendent into the immanent, does Jantzen endow the vagaries of human preference with a kind of permanence? Is everything reducible to human desire and action?

An alternative approach to transcendence and immanence is found in Patrice Haynes' theological materialism. Haynes draws upon the classical formulation of the transcendent God. With Jantzen, she is influenced by Irigaray, but her resulting theology is different, Haynes claiming that 'theology can articulate a non-reductive materialism whereby the affirmation of divine transcendence neither inhibits the becoming of material creation nor assumes that pure, self-forming activity must be the hallmark of lively matter' (2014b, 143). As Annie Dillard says: 'not only is God immanent in everything, but more profoundly everything is simultaneously in God, within God the transcendent. There is divine, not just bushes' (1999, 176–7).

A further aspect of Haynes' account of transcendence is helpful for my approach, as she 'challenge[s] an uncritical humanism' (2014b, 143). Her God is one whose 'agency is wholly unique and, thus, cannot be contrasted with the agencies of this world, or with the agency of the world itself' (2014b, 143). Becoming is supplemented with an emphasis on 'the *coming to be* of matter' (2014b, 143). This latter concept highlights the sheer givenness of life, while challenging any account that makes God a cipher for the act of human becoming. Rather, 'God grants each thing its space to be and become' (2014b, 143).

The anthropomorphic framing of God disappears, and with it the traditional framing of the 'problem' of evil. At this point, Stewart Sutherland's revisionist theism becomes relevant, as he places the question of what grounds the ethical life centre stage. Sutherland begins with the problem of evil and suffering: taking seriously its reality must lead to the rejection of God as a being like ourselves only greater. But this does not mean that the idea of God loses its power: far from it. Released from the millstone of anthropomorphism, the language of theism is freed up to address questions of how to live well. 'God' is reframed as a way of living made possible by 'how the world is seen when it is seen *sub specie aeternitatis*' (1984, 99). A similar idea can be identified in Weil's approval of Taoism's depiction of the divine as 'The Way' (Little 1988, 57). A fundamental connection is made between the divine and the question of how to live.

Sutherland directs attention to the nature of the physical world. Far from reflecting a crude Darwinism that ignores the possibility of bravery or self-sacrifice or justice, the fact that such ways of living *are* possible opens up reflection on the nature of the universe that supports such values. Willem Drees expresses the benefit of this kind of revised theism, for the questions to which theism traditionally directed attention are 'too important to be disregarded'. These are questions 'about existence, the fact that somehow our world with its regularities seems given, and the question about values and perfection, *beyond the biases of human self-interests and limitations*' (Drees 2016, 197; my emphasis). It is the latter point that lies at the heart of Sutherland's ethical project. The divine – the way of life that is *sub specie aeternitatis* – offers 'the hope, and indeed the belief, that there is an understanding of the affairs of men

[sic] that is not relative to the outlook of individual, community or age' (1984, 88). This anchoring is necessary if our obligations to each other are not to be eroded by the (not-infrequently selfish) preferences of human beings and the workings of the will-to-power.

If Jantzen's divine is anchored in the creation of human subjectivity, a different hope informs the ideas of Sutherland and Drees. God is a lived reality, 'a way of being in the world' (Pattison 2018, 71); but this way of being transcends the human, for it indicates a fundamental feature of the universe that will survive, *regardless of the fate of humanity itself.* This is the additional hope to which Sutherland draws attention. Values are not created solely by human beings. When he frames the life lived 'under a kind of eternity', he highlights the possibility that 'such a view is not even relative to the outlook of mankind [sic]' (1984, 88). Another kind of orientation is possible: away from human preferences towards consideration of the world, of life, of 'God' itself. A new framing for an ethic of flourishing becomes possible. Weil describes this in words that inform the argument of the next section. We are 'to empty ourselves of our false divinity, to deny ourselves, *to give up being the centre of the world in imagination*' (1959, 115; my emphasis). This radical de-centring of the human opens up new vistas for feminist philosophy of religion. This is made possible by revisiting the phenomenon of 'natural' evil: a seemingly unpromising, yet ultimately helpful, gateway to an account of flourishing that resists the self-centredness of individualism, while valuing the the physical world itself.

3.3 Revisiting 'Natural Evil': Embracing the Physical World

Feminists challenge the construction of natural forces as evil on the grounds that this reflects a false binary between humans and the natural world (Ortner 1972; Plumwood 1993). Rather than reject the category of natural evil, I want to suggest that consideration of the themes revolving around it open up reflection on what it means to flourish as a human being, while placing at the heart of a feminist philosophy of religion renewed consideration of the importance of the physical world. Understanding human beings as part of an ecosystem requires resistance to constructions of the human as somehow detached from the rest of the physical world. More complex, interwoven understandings of 'natural evil', that pay attention to the realities of this holistic vision, make *de-centring* the human an important part of a revised feminist philosophy of religion.

Accepting humans as part of an integrated ecosystem need not ignore the differences between human and other forms of life. Ellen Armour's case study of Hurricane Katrina reveals the difficulties of separating natural forces from human decision-making. When Katrina devastated the southern United States in August 2005, suffering arose, not just from the event of the hurricane itself, but from the failures of governmental responses to the emergency. As Armour's analysis reveals, attitudes to race and economic class contributed to the suffering that arose from a seemingly 'natural' phenomenon. Katrina was 'as much a social as a physical catastrophe; it is an (un)making shaped as much by human action and inaction as by natural forces' (Armour 2016, 183). Falling back on a simple binary division between moral and natural evil cannot explain the events surrounding Katrina. Hurricanes are not 'evil', even if they bring suffering to human beings. They are part of the processes of a living planet; and as climate change is revealing, they are forces being shaped by human actions.

Good reasons remain, however, for retaining the category of natural evil, albeit in a way rather different from its role in theodical arguments. There, natural events that bring with them considerable suffering – principally, but not only, to human beings (Rowe 1979, 337) – bring in their wake problems for a God constructed as an agent who created this world. If *we* would act to ameliorate suffering, why doesn't God? Anthropocentrism also contributes to the problem. If, following Feuerbach, the concept of God reflects human values, a special place is assigned to the human, reflected in the image of God. Processes that impact negatively on the human are then rendered 'obviously evil' because they challenge the centrality and importance of the human.

An alternative way of proceeding is to consider the way events designated as forms of natural evil destabilise the hierarchical relationship between humans and nature on which this category depends. If human beings are part of a web of life, the reality of human vulnerability comes to the fore. Rather than beings defined by independence, we are dependent on a network of relationships and the world itself. The events we formulate as 'natural evils' prompt different questions when filtered through the imperative for finding ways of living that enable human flourishing *within the context* of this fragile world.

A new way of envisioning humanity is required to make this move. Weil describes the human predicament in a phrase that shapes my reflections: 'we live in a world of unreality and dreams' (1959, 115). 'To see the true light and hear the true silence' – to understand ourselves correctly in the world – requires that we 'give up our imaginary position as the centre, to renounce it, not only intellectually but in the imaginative part of our soul' (1959, 115). These words are of utmost importance for feminist philosophers of religion. We might *intellectually* reject the anthropocentrism that misrepresents the place of human beings in the broader cosmos, but have far more difficulty giving up the centrality of the human in our *imaginations* and the ideas we formulate.

For this reason, attending to natural evil is important because it enables a recalibration of our perspective. In natural phenomena (earthquakes, hurricanes, volcanoes, illness, death), formulated as 'evil' because of their adverse effects on human life, we run up against the limits of human wishing. That we are physical bodies, intimately connected to and shaped by a physical world, is not a fact to be evaded but accepted, perhaps even embraced. The feminism that starts from this premise must resist ideas of the human centred on accounts of subjectivity that render the body as little more than malleable matter. Desires to master the self are not far from desires for mastery over the world itself.

Disrupting ideas of mastery does not mean evading responsibility for the effect human actions have on the subtle balances of the ecosystem. As Arendt notes, the ability of human beings to create is caught up in the image of *homo faber*, where a radical distinction is made between human action and the world it seeks to shape. The capacity for industry is not an unmitigated good, and Arendt's analysis establishes, instead, the *vita activa* (the active life), which has at its heart 'love for the world' (1998 [1958], 324). Human creativity is best placed within the limits imposed by the physical. We are fleshy beings who can hurt and be hurt. We may not like this; we may kick against this; but we are mortal beings, dependent on a physical world, who suffer and die. Without the flourishing of the world, our ability to flourish is impossible.

Jantzen's emphasis on natality and Anderson's later preoccupation with the possibilities of 'enhancing life'[16] suggest the importance of this focus for feminist philosophy of religion. My reflections on life are shaped differently from theirs, and reflect a desire to challenge accounts of human subjectivity that pay insufficient attention to the physical world that enables human flourishing. Predrag Cicovacki's reclamation of Albert Schweitzer's ethical vision (2012) offers a helpful framework, offering fertile ground for a feminist philosophy of religion focused on resisting the differing forms anthropocentrism may take.

Schweitzer's reflections were formed by the context of the 1920s, a post-war period of considerable upheaval. They fit, as a result, rather well with the context framing the writing of this Element: the shadow of the Global Financial Crisis of 2008, and the Covid-19 Pandemic of 2020–21. Schweitzer is dissatisfied with the philosophy of his day, for it has failed to provide a compelling worldview, effectively reducing itself to 'largely the history of philosophy' (1959 [1923], 7). He aims to correct this by providing a theory of the universe 'which gives existence the preference as against non-existence and thus affirms life as something possessing value in itself' (1959 [1923], 57). He

---

[16] The title of the John Templeton Foundation project (September 2014 to August 2017), with which Anderson was involved.

directs attention to the 'will-to-live', the *feeling* of life that flows through all living beings. This is more than phenomenological, for it opens up the arena for ethics. We should start our reflections from the experience of life: 'what is decisive for our life-view is not our knowledge of the world but the certainty of the volition which is given in our will-to-live'. The experience of life, flowing through us, directs us to those with whom we share this world and this feeling of life: '*the eternal spirit meets us in nature as mysterious creative power.* In our will-to-live we experience it within us as volition which is both world- and life-affirming and ethical' (1959 [1923], 78).

How he makes the move to the ethical is telling. Reverence for life is grounded in the connection to be made between the feeling of life in our bodies and the rest of the living world: 'Ethics grow out of the same root as world- and life-affirmation, for ethics, too, are nothing but reverence for life. This is what gives me the fundamental principle of morality, namely, that good consists in maintaining, promoting, and enhancing life, and that destroying, injuring, and limiting life are evil' (1959 [1923], 79).

Just as we value the life of our own bodies, so we must make an imaginative connection to the lives of all others: human and non-human. The value of *being alive* thus forms the basis for his understanding of the sacred and for his ethic of how to live well. We are returned to the physical and, crucially, to the experiences of the body. Schweitzer's is thus a grounded ethic that requires resistance to the thinking Weil defines as the imagination of the centre. The life that runs through our veins is not unique to human beings but connects us to all the varied forms of life making up the cosmos. Weil's impersonal account of the divine sits rather well with this. It is life, and crucially *the shared experience of life*, that opens up reflection on our connection to that which transcends the human realm: the universe (God) itself.

Schweitzer's ethic centres on doing 'everything in our power to prevent suffering' (1959 [1923], 30). *All* life should be treated with respect, even when we kill it for food or in order to safeguard other lives. With Arendt and Minnich, this demands the cultivation of thoughtful practice: 'Don't destroy out of thoughtlessness' (1959 [1923], 26). Schweitzer is no naive sentimentalist; he is fully aware that 'nature knows no reverence for life' (1988 [1919], 15). The horrors of the natural world are not avoided: 'nature leads ants to band together and to attack a small creature and hound it to death' (1988 [1919], 15). *But acknowledging these horrors makes the human ability to lessen suffering even more imperative.*

Schweitzer's is not an easy vision of life or how to live well. It might be difficult to connect his reflections on the feeling of life with Weil's grounding of the ethical in the love of God. There is certainly a tension between the two claims, but that very tension indicates something important. The desire for coherence can slide into acceptance of the simplistic binaries that create the problem of evil in the first place: the world is either 'good' or it is 'evil'; it is either the creation of God or it is not; God either cares or 'He' doesn't. More complex accounts of the divine are offered by Weil, Sutherland and Drees, and, at its best, religion does not avoid such complexity, but seeks to hold it together: 'in the midst of life, we are in death'; the torture of the Cross is the path to resurrection; the Buddhist claim that all is suffering. The teeming world of the struggle and celebration of life is met by the human ability to connect to that shared life *and* to live differently: to be loving, self-sacrificing, self-renouncing, altruistic. For Schweitzer, a religious sensibility is required to anchor the reverence for life: 'every being must be holy for us' (1959 [1923], 26). An eternal perspective is required to enable this step: a perspective that grapples with the tensions of life and accepts that faith and ethics are far from straightforward.

Schweitzer's ethic resists the temptation to make human beings central to the imagination. The concern with personal transformation that pervades the spiritual turn in feminist philosophy of religion is not altogether amenable to the reorientation of ourselves towards the universe required by Schweitzer and Weil. Rediscovering the significance of the body opens up new vistas for a feminist politics, and it also enables the feminist philosopher of religion to consider models of the divine that help foster new ways of being in the world.

My argument thus comes full circle. A feminist philosophy of religion is required that disrupts binary thinking, that attends to the practice of living, and that is anchored in reflections on the value of life itself. This kind of reflection urges us to move out of our self-centredness and into a place where we might embrace the connection between ourselves and other forms of life in all their variety and diversity. Feminist thinking thus makes possible new ways of seeing the world and others.

4 Principles for a Practical Feminist Philosophy of Religion

The sheer range of themes covered in this Element suggest something of the possibilities that come with revisiting Anderson and Jantzen's foundational works in feminist philosophy of religion. I have developed their ideas in my attempt at constructing a practical feminist philosophy of religion. Far from being the final word on this subject, I hope I have provided a sense of how this practical approach can shape a philosophy of religion in response to some of the dominant concerns of our age. Feminist philosophy is at its best when it seeks to address the problems of human relationships and how more flourishing forms of living might be established. To further that endeavour, I suggest three principles for future work:

Firstly, critique is a central aspect of feminist work in philosophy. I have suggested that this critical work address the importance of truth and the necessity of self-criticism. The struggle for truth is foundational for the ethical life. At the same time, the temptation of ideological purity must be resisted. Both make good conversation vital for the creation of flourishing public spaces. Thinking 'we' are obviously right and have nothing to learn from 'them' is one of the problems of contemporary identity politics. The critique made by black feminists of white feminists opened up the significance of self-criticism, and this must be extended. *All* of us are fallible: to start from this position makes possible more creative and honest spaces for thought. My desire is for a philosophy of religion that enables the cultivation of better relationships on the basis of the common humanity and world that we share, and that, at its best, religious practice attempts to establish.

Acknowledging the need for self-criticism leads to my second point. A practical feminist philosophy of religion embraces the creative power of diverse perspectives for better conversations and seeks to enshrine them by extending access to education for all. At the same time, the desire for diversity must extend to the sources for our philosophies. Our ideas should not be constrained by adherence to one group of thinkers; rather, we should seek allies who enable creative thinking. There is scope for conversations across the ages and with thinkers from different places. Feminist philosophy of religion cannot afford to be shaped by insularity and exclusion. What matters is finding conversation partners who, through challenge or support, help us nurture a flourishing world.

Finally, a practical feminist philosophy of religion is an active philosophy. I started with the claim that feminism is a political movement, and the investigation of evil bears this out. Philosophy of religion can be shaped as a form of critical practice directed at establishing a flourishing world: the search for truth and the cultivation of honesty are thus fundamental components for the ethical life. A feminism configured on these principles, shaped by an awareness of ourselves as part of an ecosystem, makes possible flourishing ways of living: for human beings, and also for our home, the Earth.

References

Adkins L (2002) *Revisions: Gender and Sexuality in Late Modernity.* Buckingham: Open University Press.

Anderson PS (1993) *Ricoeur and Kant.* Atlanta, GA: Scholars Press.

Anderson PS (1998) *A Feminist Philosophy of Religion.* Oxford: Blackwell.

Anderson PS (2009) 'A thoughtful love of life': a spiritual turn in philosophy of religion. *Svensk Teologisk Kvartalskrift* **85**, 119–29.

Anderson PS (2012) *Re-visioning Gender in Philosophy of Religion: Reason, Love and Epistemic Locatedness.* Farnham: Ashgate.

Anderson PS (2021 [2016]) Silencing and speaker vulnerability: undoing an oppressive form of (wilful) ignorance. In Goulimari P (ed.), *Love and Vulnerability: Thinking with Pamela Sue Anderson.* London: Routledge, pp. 34–43.

Anderson PS and Clack B (eds.) (2004) *Feminist Philosophy of Religion: Critical Readings.* London: Routledge.

Arendt H (1968 [1948]) *The Origins of Totalitarianism.* New York: Harcourt.

Arendt H (1998 [1958]) *The Human Condition.* Chicago: University of Chicago Press.

Arendt H (1964) *Eichmann in Jerusalem: A Report on the Banality of Evil.* Harmondsworth: Penguin.

Armour ET (1999) *Deconstruction, Feminist Theology and the Problem of Difference: Subverting the Race/Gender Divide.* Chicago: University of Chicago Press.

Armour ET (2016) *Signs and Wonders: Theology after Modernity.* New York: Columbia University Press.

Armour ET (2018) Transing the study of religion: a Christian theological response. *Journal of Feminist Studies in Religion* **34**, 58–63.

Armour ET and St Ville S (eds.) (2006) *Bodily Citations: Religion and Judith Butler.* New York: Columbia Press.

Ayer AJ (1971 [1936]) *Language, Truth and Logic.* Harmondsworth: Penguin.

Barth K (2014 [1934]) No! Answer to Emil Brunner. In Fraenkel P (ed.), *Natural Theology.* Eugene, OR: Wipf and Stock, 65–128.

Beattie T (2004) Redeeming Mary: the potential of Marian symbolism for feminist philosophy of religion. In Anderson PS and Clack B (eds.), *Feminist Philosophy of Religion: Critical Readings.* London: Routledge, pp. 107–22.

Beauvoir S d (1972 [1949]) *The Second Sex.* London: Penguin.

Bellah R (1964) Religious evolution. *American Sociological Review* **29**, 358–74.

Bonhoeffer D (1971 [1953]) *Letter and Papers from Prison.* London: SCM Press.

Braithwaite RB (1971 [1955]) An empiricist's view of the nature of religious belief. In Mitchell B (ed.), *The Philosophy of Religion.* Oxford: Oxford University Press, pp. 72–91.

Brennan S (2009) Feminist ethics and everyday inequalities. *Hypatia* **24**, 141–59.

Browne V (2014) *Feminism, Time and Nonlinear History.* London: Palgrave Macmillan.

Brownmiller S (1975) *Against Our Will.* New York: Simon and Schuster.

Burley M (2020) *A Radical Pluralist Philosophy of Religion.* London: Bloomsbury.

Butler J (2006 [1990]) *Gender Trouble.* London: Routledge.

Butler J (2006) *Precarious Life: The Powers of Mourning and Violence.* London: Verso.

Butler J (2014) *Bodies That Matter: On the Discursive Limits of 'Sex'.* London: Routledge.

Cameron D and Frazer E (1987) *The Lust to Kill.* New York: New York University Press.

Card C (2005) *The Atrocity Paradigm.* Oxford: Oxford University Press.

Card C (2010) *Confronting Evils: Terrorism, Torture, Genocide.* Cambridge: Cambridge University Press.

Carrette J (2006) Bringing philosophy to life: a review article in memory of Grace M Jantzen. *Literature and Theology* **20**, 321–5.

Christ C (1979) Why women need the Goddess. In Christ C P and Plaskow J (eds.), *Womanspirit Rising: A Feminist Reader on Religion.* San Francisco, CA: Harper & Row, pp. 273–87.

Christ CP (2003) *She Who Changes.* London: Palgrave Macmillan.

Cicovacki P (2012) *The Restoration of Albert Schweitzer's Ethical Vision.* London: Bloomsbury.

Clack B (1999) *Misogyny in the Western Philosophical Tradition: A Critical Reader.* London: Macmillan.

Clack B (2018) Evil, feminism and a philosophy of transformation. In Trakakis N (ed.), *The Problem of Evil: Eight Views in Dialogue.* Oxford: Oxford University Press, pp. 123–50.

Coakley S (2002) *Powers and Submissions: Spirituality, Philosophy and Gender.* Oxford: Blackwell.

Collins PH (1990) *Black Feminist Thought.* London: Routledge.

Collins PH (1996) What's in a name? Womanism, black feminism and beyond. *The Black Scholar* **26**, 9–17.

Collins PH and Bilge S (2020) *Intersectionality*. London: Bloomsbury.

Cone J (1990) *A Black Theology of Liberation*. Maryknoll, NY: Orbis Books.

Crenshaw K (2017) *On Intersectionality: Essential Writings*. New York: New Press.

Daly M (1978) *Gyn/Ecology: The Metaethics of Radical Feminism*. Boston, MA: Beacon Press.

Daly M (1986 [1973]) *Beyond God the Father*. Boston, MA: Beacon Press.

Day K (2016) *Religious Resistance to Neoliberalism: Womanist and Black Feminist Perspectives*. London: Palgrave Macmillan.

DiCenzo M (2014) 'Our freedom and its results': measuring progress in the aftermath of suffrage. *Women's History Review* **23**, 421–40.

Dillard A (1999) *For the Time Being*. New York: Vintage.

Drees W (2016) The divine as ground of existence and of transcendental values: an exploration. In Buckareff A and Nagasawa Y (eds.), *Alternative Concepts of God: Essays on the Metaphysics of the Divine*. Oxford: Oxford University Press, pp. 195–212.

Dworkin A (1981) *Pornography: Men Possessing Women*. London: The Women's Press.

Eliade M (1959) *The Sacred and the Profane: The Nature of Religion*. New York: Harcourt Brace.

Ellis AJ *et al* (2020) New hope or old futures in disguise? Neoliberalism, the Covid-19 pandemic and the possibility for social change. *International Journal of Sociology and Social Policy* **40**, 831–48.

Flax J (1995) Race/gender and the ethics of difference: a reply to Okin's 'gender inequality and cultural differences'. *Political Theory* **23**, 500–10.

Frank A (2002 [1991]) *At the Will of the Body: Reflections on Illness*. New York: Houghton Mifflin Harcourt.

Frankl V (2004) *Man's Search for Meaning*. London: Rider.

Freud S (1907) Obsessional practices and religious rituals. In Strachey J (ed.), *Standard Edition of the Works of Sigmund Freud Volume 9*. London: Hogarth Press, pp.115–27.

Freud S (1919) The 'uncanny'. In Strachey J (ed.), *Standard Edition of the Works of Sigmund Freud Volume 17*. London: Hogarth Press, pp.217–56.

Fricker M (1994) Knowledge as construct: theorising the role of gender in knowledge. In Lennon K and Whitford M (eds.), *Knowing the Difference: Feminist Perspectives on Epistemology*. London: Routledge, pp. 95–109.

Gamble S (1998) *Companion to Feminism and Post-Feminism*. London: Routledge.

Geddes J (2003) Banal evil and useless knowledge: Hannah Arendt and Charlotte Delbo on evil after the Holocaust. *Hypatia* **18**, 104–15.

Goulimari P (ed.) (2021) *Love and Vulnerability: Thinking with Pamela Sue Anderson*. London: Routledge.

Grant J (1989) *White Women's Christ and Black Women's Jesus: Feminist Christology and Womanist Response*. Atlanta, GA: Scholars Press.

Hallie P (1979) *Lest Innocent Blood Be Shed*. New York: HarperCollins.

Hamilton K (1965) Homo religiosus and historical faith. *Journal of American Academy of Religion* **33**, 213–22.

Hampson D (1990) *Theology and Feminism*. Oxford: Blackwell.

Hampson D (ed.) (1996) *Swallowing a Fishbone? Feminist Theologians Debate Christianity*. London: SCM Press.

Hampson D (2002) *After Christianity*. London: SCM Press.

Haraway D (1991) *Simians, Cyborgs, and Women: The Reinvention of Nature*. London: Routledge.

Harding S (1993) Rethinking standpoint epistemology: what is 'strong objectivity'? In Alcoff L and Potter E (eds.), *Feminist Epistemologies*. London: Routledge, pp. 49–82.

Harris H (2004) Struggling for truth. In Anderson PS and Clack B (eds.), *Feminist Philosophy of Religion: Critical Readings*. London: Routledge, pp. 73–86.

Harvey D (2005) *A Brief History of Neoliberalism*. Oxford: Oxford University Press.

Haynes P (2014a) Transcendence, materialism and the reenchantment of nature: toward a theological materialism. In Howie G and Jobling J (eds.), *Women and the Divine: Touching Transcendence*. London: Palgrave Macmillan, pp. 55–78.

Haynes P (2014b) Creative becoming and the patiency of matter: feminism, new materialism and theology. *Angelaki* **19**, 131–50.

Heidegger M (1983 [1947]) *Basic Writings*. London: Routledge.

Hekman S (2014) *The Feminine Subject*. Cambridge: Polity Press.

Hesiod (1988) *Theogony and Works and Days*. Translated by ML West. Oxford: Oxford University Press.

Hewitt S and Scrutton A (2018) Philosophy and living religion: an introduction. *International Journal of Philosophy and Theology* **79**, 349–54.

Hick J (1989) *An Interpretation of Religion*. Basingstoke: Macmillan.

Hollywood A (2004) Practice, belief and feminist philosophy of religion. In Anderson PS and Clack B (eds.), *Feminist Philosophy of Religion: Critical Readings*. London: Routledge, pp. 225–40.

hooks b (1982) *Ain't I a Woman: Black Women and Feminism*. London: Pluto Press.

hooks b (2000) *Where We Stand: Class Matters*. London: Routledge.

Hume D (1998 [1779]) *Dialogues Concerning Natural Religion*. Indianapolis, IN: Hackett.

Jantzen G (1984) *God's World, God's Body*. London: Darton, Longman and Todd.

Jantzen G (1996) What's the difference? Knowledge and gender in (post) modern philosophy of religion. *Religious Studies* **32**, 431–48.

Jantzen G (1998) *Becoming Divine: Towards a Feminist Philosophy of Religion*. Manchester: Manchester University Press.

Kakutani M (2018) *Death of Truth: Notes on Falsehood in the Age of Trump*. London: Penguin.

Le Doeuff M (2003) *The Sex of Knowing*. New York: Routledge.

Le Doeuff M (2007 [1989]) *Hipparchia's Choice*. New York: Columbia University Press.

Lemke T (2001) The birth of bio-politics: Michel Foucault's lecture at the Collège de France on neo-liberal governmentality. *Economy and Society* **30**, 190–207.

Little JP (1988) *Simone Weil: Waiting on Truth*. Oxford: Berg.

Lloyd G (1984) *The Man of Reason*. London: Methuen.

Lloyd M (2005) *Beyond Identity Politics: Feminism, Power and Politics*. London: Sage.

Mackie JL (1955) Evil and omnipotence. *Mind* **64**, 200–12.

Mahmood S (2001) Feminist theory, embodiment, and the docile agent: some reflections on the Egyptian Islamic revival. *Cultural Anthropology* **16**, 202–36.

Mantel H (2020) *The Mirror and the Light*. London: Fourth Estate.

Mawson T (2005) *Belief in God*. Oxford: Oxford University Press.

McCord Adams M (1999) *Horrendous Evils and the Goodness of God*. Ithaca, NY: Cornell University Press.

McNay L (1992) *Foucault and Feminism: Power, Gender, and the Self*. Evanston, IL: Northwestern University Press.

Midgley M (1984) *Wickedness*. London: Ark.

Miller D (1966) 'Homo religiosus' and the death of God. *Journal of Bible and Religion* **34**, 305–15.

Minnich E (2017) *The Evil of Banality*. London: Rowman & Littlefield.

Mirowski P (2014) *Never Let a Serious Crisis Go To Waste: How Neoliberalism Survived the Financial Meltdown*. London: Verso.

Moltmann J (1973) *The Crucified God*. London: SCM Press.

Morin R and Cohen D (2018) Guiliani: 'Truth Isn't Truth'. Available from www.politico.com/story/2018/08/19/giuliani-truth-todd-trump-788161 (accessed 6 March 2021).

Nagasawa Y (2018) Response to Clack. In Trakakis N (ed.), *The Problem of Evil: Eight Views in Dialogue*. Oxford: Oxford University Press, pp. 138–9.

Neale RS (1967) Working-class women and women's suffrage. *Labour History* **12**, 16–34.

Nelson L (1999) Bodies (and spaces) do matter: the limits of performativity. *Gender, Place and Culture* **6**, 331–53.

Newman A (1994) Feminist social criticism and Marx's theory of religion. *Hypatia* **9**, 15–37.

Nicholson L (2010) Feminism in "waves": useful metaphor or not? *New Politics* **12**. Available from https://newpol.org/issue_post/feminism-waves-useful-metaphor-or-not/ (accessed 10 March 2021).

Nietzsche F (1969 [1883–5]) *Thus Spoke Zarathustra*. Harmondsworth: Penguin.

Nietzsche F (1998 [1886]) *Beyond Good and Evil*. Oxford: Oxford University Press.

Nixon J (2015) *Hannah Arendt and the Politics of Friendship*. London: Bloomsbury.

Noddings N (1989) *Women and Evil*. Berkeley: University of California Press.

Nussbaum M (1999) The professor of parody: the hip, defeatist feminism of Judith Butler. *New Republic* **220**, 37–44.

Oborne P (2021) *The Assault on Truth*. London: Simon & Schuster.

O'Brien CC (2015 [1972]) *The Suspecting Glance*. London: Faber & Faber.

Okin SM (1998) Feminism and multiculturalism: some tensions. *Ethics* **108**, 661–84.

Ortner S (1972) Is female to male as nature is to culture? *Feminist Studies* **1**, 5–31.

Pagels E (1989) *Adam, Eve and the Serpent*. New York: Vintage.

Panchuk M (2019) That we may be whole: doing philosophy of religion with the whole self. In Panchuk M, Hereth B and Timpe K (eds.), *The Lost Sheep in Philosophy of Religion: Essays on Disability, Gender, Race and Animals*. New York: Routledge, pp. 55–76.

Pattison G (2018) *A Phenomenology of the Devout Life: A Philosophy of Christian Life, Part 1*. Oxford: Oxford University Press.

Peck J (2010) Zombie neoliberalism and the ambidextrous state. *Theoretical Criminology* **14**, 104–10.

Perez CC (2019) *Invisible Women: Exposing Data Bias in a World Designed by Men*. London: Chatto & Windus.

Plumwood V (1993) *Feminism and the Mastery of Nature*. London: Routledge.

Raphael M (1996) *Thealogy and Embodiment: The Post-Patriarchal Reconstruction of Female Sacrality*. Sheffield: Sheffield Academic Press.

Raphael M (2003) *The Female Face of God in Auschwitz*. London: Routledge.

Rohr R (2018) *A Spring within Us*. London: SPCK.

Rose N (1999) *Governing the Soul: The Shaping of the Private Self*. London: Free Association.

Roth J (1981) A theodicy of protest. In Davis S (ed.), *Encountering Evil*. Edinburgh: T & T Clark, pp. 7–22.

Rowe W (1979) The problem of evil and some varieties of atheism. *American Philosophical Quarterly* **16**, 335–41.

Ruether RR (1983) *Sexism and God-Talk: Toward a Feminist Theology*. London: SCM.

Ruether RR (2012) *Women and Redemption: A Theological History*. Minneapolis, MN: Fortress Press.

Sanders LS (2007) 'Feminists love a utopia': collaboration, conflict and the futures of feminism. In Howie G and Mumford R (eds.), *Third Way Feminism: A Critical Exploration*. London: Palgrave Macmillan, pp. 3–15.

Saul J (2013) Implicit bias, stereotype threat, and women in philosophy. In Hutchison K and Jenkins F (eds.), *Women in Philosophy: What Needs to Change?* Oxford: Oxford University Press, pp. 39–60.

Schweitzer A (1959 [1923]) *The Philosophy of Civilisation*. New York: Macmillan.

Schweitzer A (1988 [1919]) *A Place for Revelation*. London: Macmillan.

Soelle D (1975) *Suffering*. London: DLT.

Stanton CS (2016 [1895]) *The Women's Bible*. Scotts Valley, CA: CreateSpace Publishing.

Stock K (2021) *Material Girls: Why Reality Matters for Feminism*. London: Fleet.

Stump E (2010) *Wandering in Darkness: Narrative and the Problem of Suffering*. Oxford: Oxford University Press.

Sutherland S (1984) *God, Jesus and Belief*. Oxford: Blackwell.

Taliaferro C and Griffiths P (eds) (2003) *Philosophy of Religion: An Anthology*. Oxford: Blackwell.

Thomas R, Eliot O and Clark D (2021) UK gender pay gap widens despite pressure on business to improve. Available from www.ft.com/content/239c95cc-d34f-43e9-a61e-faa7954277b6 (accessed 11 October 2021).

Tillich P (1965) *Theology of Culture*. Oxford: Oxford University Press.

Tillich P (1977 [1952]) *The Courage to Be*. Glasgow: Fount.

Townes E (2006) *Womanist Ethics and the Cultural Production of Evil*. London: Palgrave Macmillan.

Wade C (2020) Coercive control post-Challen'. Available from www.counselma gazine.co.uk/articles/coercive-control-post-challen (accessed 16 March 2021).

Warner M (1990 [1976]) *Alone of All Her Sex: The Myth and Cult of the Virgin Mary*. London: Picador.

Weil S (1952) *The Need for Roots*. London: Routledge & Kegan Paul.

Weil S (1959) *Waiting on God*. London: Fontana.

Welch S (1989) *Feminist Ethic of Risk*. Minneapolis: Fortress.

Williams B (2002) *Truth and Truthfulness*. Princeton, NJ: Princeton University Press.

Williams D (1993) *Sisters in the Wilderness: The Challenge of Womanist God-Talk*. Maryknoll, NY: Orbis Books.

Cambridge Elements ≡

Philosophy of Religion

Yujin Nagasawa

University of Birmingham

Yujin Nagasawa is Professor of Philosophy and Co-Director of the John Hick Centre for Philosophy of Religion at the University of Birmingham. He is currently President of the British Society for the Philosophy of Religion. He is a member of the Editorial Board of *Religious Studies*, the *International Journal for Philosophy of Religion* and *Philosophy Compass*.

About the Series

This Cambridge Elements series provides concise and structured introductions to all the central topics in the philosophy of religion. It offers balanced, comprehensive coverage of multiple perspectives in the philosophy of religion. Contributors to the series are cutting-edge researchers who approach central issues in the philosophy of religion. Each provides a reliable resource for academic readers and develops new ideas and arguments from a unique viewpoint.

Cambridge Elements ≡

Philosophy of Religion

.

Printed in the United States
by Baker & Taylor Publisher Services